MESSED UP

RECALCULATE THE DIRECTION OF YOUR LIFE AND FIND YOUR WAY FORWARD

JULIE SCHAECHER

Quantity sales special discounts are available on quantity purchases by corporations, associations, and others. For details, contact the publisher at the address above.

Orders by U.S. trade bookstores and wholesalers.
Email info@ BeyondPublishing.net

The Beyond Publishing Speakers Bureau can bring authors to your live event. For more information or to book an event contact the Beyond Publishing Speakers Bureau speak@BeyondPublishing.net

The Author can be reached directly at BeyondPublishing.net

Creative contribution by Carol McManus.

Cover Design - Low & Joe Creative, Brea, CA 92821
Illustrations - Whitnee Nixon, Tall Tale Studios

Manufactured and printed in the United States of America distributed globally by BeyondPublishing.net

BEYOND
PUBLISHING

New York | Los Angeles | London | Sydney

ISBN Hardcover: 978-1-637921-74-6

ISBN Softcover: 978-1-637921-75-3

DEDICATED TO

The amazing Mr. Schaecher who dared to believe in the possibility of us. Thank you for your courageous love and for faithfully accepting the challenge.

The many friends and family members who encouraged me for years to write it all down. Thank you for believing that there is value in the telling of our stories.

In loving memory of Clarice Jepsen who opened up her home and her heart to so many of us who struggled to understand what it meant to be loved unconditionally. I am forever grateful for the time she took to tell me about a God who would never give up on me.

CONTENTS

INTRODUCTION

Life is messy!

Maybe you believe that your mistakes have messed things up for good, and you can't imagine a way out of the mess you've made. Or perhaps, someone else made a big mess of things, and your life got in the way. Regardless, if you picked up this book, there is a very good chance you have situations in your life you think are beyond repair. By the end of our journey together, you will think differently.

Since the beginning of time, humans have been notorious for making a mess of things. Take Adam and Eve, for example: most would agree they made quite a mess of a pretty-sweet situation. The good news is, no matter how broken, confused, or hopeless things may seem, we can be confident that God's desire to bless our lives is greater than our ability to mess things up.

Maybe you agree that God can help, but you question why in the world would He want to? I have great news. God has not changed his mind about you. You were inspired in His heart before you ever took a breath. In fact, the Bible says He knew who you would be before He formed you in your mother's womb, and you were purposefully made to live out His inspired destiny. If you can dare to believe this, you will see how God's good plan for you can prevail over the challenging circumstances in your life.

You may not believe in yourself at this moment, but here is the really great news: it's not all about you. Now, I say that in the kindest way possible, and I want to remind you that...

His grace is all you need, and His power works
best in our weakness.
(2 Cor. 12:9)

This is where our confidence lies – not in our efforts or successes or failures, but in His goodness and power and love. Maybe you have heard this a thousand times before, but have you learned to walk in the truth of it? If not, I believe you can.

Right now, you might be asking yourself why you should listen to me. I am certainly no theologian, but I have a God story to tell you. If you have ever heard me speak, you know I did everything in my power to mess up my life, and how I got here is nothing short of a miracle. I often say that my bio should read:

Divorced, single mom by the age of 20, two-time college dropout, former alcoholic, drug abuser, and cocaine dealer, and living proof that there really is no lost cause. Oh, and by the way, I'm a pastor. Maybe that isn't a reason to continue reading, but I hope you do.

Some would say I had not been dealt a favorable hand of cards. I was not born into a broken home in the traditional sense, but there were many things that were broken in my life as a child. As a first-generation American, whose father came from

Mexico in the early 1950s, I was raised in an environment caught between two cultures. I was one of dozens of cousins, not the oldest, not the youngest, not the smartest or the most talented. Poverty, abuse, drug addiction, and violence were such a part of my childhood that they did not seem abnormal, and it would not be until I was well into adulthood that I would begin to realize the effect they had on shaping what I believed about myself. Talk about an identity crisis. Have you ever felt like you were lost in the midst of your own life?

Despite these challenges, there was something in me as a child that dared my heart to believe I was something very special. In the grand scheme of things, I somehow mattered. As a young girl, I was driven to prove this despite my life circumstances. From the outside, you might have believed it. I worked hard to be "that girl". You know her: athlete, straight-A student, cheerleader. The girl who has everything she needs to win at life. For a moment, I might have even believed it was possible.

It was all so promising, but somewhere along the way, my life got messy. By the age of 22, I found myself a single mom with a three-year old, living with a drug-addicted, violent, and abusive man – who was not my husband or the father of my baby. To make matters worse, he was involved in dangerous large-scale drug trafficking. I had already been married once, divorced, rejected, and emotionally and physically abused. I had a mountain of debt and was not bringing in enough money on my own to survive as a single mom. Among other things, shame and pride had caused me to isolate and disconnect from family and friends, who really wanted to help me, but couldn't break through my defenses. There was little hope for the future, and I was pretty certain I would not make it out of the situation alive.

In the midst of all the craziness and for a brief minute, I actually tried to go to church, but I realized very quickly that the incredible chaos of my life was not something that most church people were prepared to deal with at that time. I get it. Messy people can be complicated, time-consuming, and oftentimes, frustrating. I never questioned God's existence, but I allowed the judgment and rejection that I felt from people to become God's voice in my head. I could see my need to accept Jesus as my Savior. I just could not believe that He could accept me. And so, I walked away.

I got very good at coping. Substance abuse and denial helped me to survive and kept me trapped in a dangerous life that I hated. Until one day, everything came crashing down. I don't mean metaphorically, I mean literally crashing down – as in, a plane crashing, falling from the sky, miraculously rescued, get-your-attention moment. It was the catalyst that would cause me to recalculate the direction of my life and begin walking the road that led to redemption and healing. Those who knew me then would have said it was an absolute impossibility, but I believe we can do impossible things. I am the girl who fell from the sky and lived to tell about it.

It's a great story. As I have shared it through the years, many have found the strength to hope again and have gained practical insight that has helped them to find a way forward and navigate lasting change in their lives.

So, how do you bounce back from failure? How do you reclaim things that were lost? How do you live with regret? How do you walk into the plan God has for your life when you have spent so much time walking away from it? How do you love the messy people in your life? If you have ever asked any of these questions, I want you to know it's possible.

I'am writing this book for the person who believes there is more. For the one who is daring to believe against all odds that things can change. For the person who, no matter how many times they fall down, they get back up. For the person who has a spark and a fire on the inside that refuses to be extinguished, and the one who is ready to fight back against the notion that the mess they are in is the best they can do.

I am not saying it will be easy. You will have to ask yourself some tough questions, get real, and change the way you think. You will have to open your heart and lay down defenses that have held you hostage for too long. You will have to hope and believe when it makes no sense that you should. If you are ready and willing, let me now encourage you to hope that all things are possible for you. I am convinced that you can find your way forward and begin to live the life that God inspired for you before you ever had the ability to mess it all up. It is within your reach, if you can dare to believe it.

"If you want to build a ship, don't drum up the men to gather wood, divide the work, and give orders. Instead, teach them to yearn for the vast and endless sea."

–Antoine de Saint-Exupéry

If you don't know where you are going,
any road will get you there.
— Lewis Carroll

Chapter 1

DARE TO BELIEVE

DARE TO BELIEVE

"Something in my life is messed up and I feel powerless to change it."

Whether we are talking about marriage, faith, parenting, career – you name it – I think we can all agree that life can be pretty messy. After decades of sitting in pastoral counseling situations with people of every age and in every station of life, I have found powerlessness to change to be a common theme, and to be the driving force behind their need for spiritual counsel.

It could be the reason you picked up this book.

You might be surprised to find yourself in a place you never thought you would be or moving in a direction you never thought you would go. Maybe it's your fault. You took a wrong turn, refused to listen to directions, or failed to pay attention to the signs that warned you not to go down that road. Or, perhaps, it is possible that someone else made a big mess of things, and your life simply got in the way.

I can relate.

I know what it's like to feel so lost you can't imagine ever finding your way again. I know what it's like to be terrified that you have destroyed any chance of becoming the person you know, deep down in your heart, you were made to be. I know what it is like to live with a mountain of regret so big, you feel you could never get beyond it. I know what it's like to watch time slip away and with it, the hope that anything in your life could still turn out the way you planned.

I used to question why God chose to use the messes of my life as a platform for His truth. I now realize this is precisely where His glory shines the brightest. There is an African proverb that says, "If the lion does not tell her story, the hunter will." We all get to decide who tells our story. I have decided it will be me. I am sure the enemy would love to tell the story of my defeat, my failure, my stupidity and selfishness, but I will tell you about victory, restoration, mercy and unbelievable grace.

God had mercy on me so that Christ Jesus could use me as a prime example of his great patience with even the worst sinners. Then others will realize that they, too, can believe in him and receive eternal life. (1 Timothy 1:16 NLT)

People have told me that my life as a young woman reads like a very bad novel. By the time I was 22, I was a divorced, single mom, living with a violent and abusive man who was not my baby's daddy. I was a two-time college dropout who could barely make it through a day without alcohol. Most of my good friends had walked away in complete frustration. I was headed for a crash. Everyone around me saw it coming. Nobody knew how to stop it.

If you were to look at my life at the time, you might not have held out much hope. In fact, statistics would say that my chances of turning things around and living a happy, successful life were pretty slim. It was obvious that I was desperately lost and in need of a major course correction in my life, but in the moment, I honestly could not see a way around the insurmountable roadblocks.

Nobody would have bet on me – including me.

There was a crash coming for sure, and I was powerless to stop it. It would prove to be the catalytic moment that changed everything for me and convinced me, beyond a shadow of a doubt, that God will never stop His pursuit of people.

There really is no lost cause.

The plane was literally running on fumes as the storm raged around the small, six-passenger aircraft. Visibility was down to 50 feet, and our landing instruments were not working, which meant we were virtually flying blind. We had been in a holding pattern while the air traffic controller at the tiny airport in northern Florida attempted to get all the planes on the ground because of a freak electrical storm. I could hear one of the two pilots speaking with the tower, "No, we didn't file a flight plan." "No, we don't have enough fuel to stay in this holding pattern." "No, we don't have any working instrumentation that can help us land this plane." An argument ensued, and the pilots began fighting – not with the tower, but with each other. At first, they were arguing about how to land the plane, which escalated into screaming, and then, they were physically fighting. The situation was quickly slipping out of control as I sat alone in the passenger section, feeling absolutely powerless to stop it.

The real truth was the plane we were in wasn't even ours. My companions had borrowed it without asking the owner, which didn't feel like stealing at the time. Apparently, there was a debt to pay. Somehow, I thought it would be a good idea to go along for the ride.

"Florida is great this time of year."

"I should take my three-year-old son, Joshua."

"We could go to Disney World."

I distinctly remember fighting with my mom as she did everything in her power to force me to leave my son at home. I was furious with her for being the killer of all fun, but I was weary of fighting. Besides, who would watch him while we went out to the clubs at night? I angrily boarded the plane without him and headed off into the unexpected storm with two cocaine dealers in the pilot seats. One of them was my live-in boyfriend, who I will refer to as my ex for the purpose of this story; the other was some random, South American drug dealer who, up to that moment, I had never seen in my life, but somehow, chose to trust to be in control of the plane he had just stolen.

I will never forget the sinking feeling of the plane cutting through the dense cloud cover as we attempted to land. The pilots were doing their best to visually spot the small runway, but every time we broke from the clouds, they would have to quickly pull up and climb back into the storm, because landing was impossible without the plane's navigation tools. We tried three times before we ran out of fuel. Then, we literally fell from the sky.

I was terrified. It was a fear unlike any other I had felt in my life, and believe me, I had lived through some scary stuff. The angry voices of the pilots and the sound of the storm were drowned out by the racing thoughts in my brain. I believed we were headed for a crash, and there was a decent chance that this was the end of my life. People rarely survive falling from the sky in an airplane.

One terrifying question dominated my thinking, "If this plane crashes, what's next?" Time seemed to slow down as I did a mental inventory of my life in the hopes of finding anything I had done that would have helped me to prepare for this moment. Did I ever even think about what's next? Did I ever make any concrete decisions about eternity? That might have been a good idea.

I was suddenly drawn to a memory, so vivid it was like a movie playing in my mind. Three years before, at the age of 19, life had taken one more very disappointing turn. I found myself alone with a newborn baby, brokenhearted, and in a situation I never thought I would be in. A well-meaning friend who tried through the years, with no success, to tell me about heaven and my need for Jesus invited me to church. Desperate for a solution to fix the mess of my life, I took him up on his offer.

This church was very different from the kind I had attended as a child – with stained glass windows, candles, and beautiful statues all around. The building was very plain. It felt more like a school auditorium with a small stage, an organ, and a simple, wooden cross hanging at the front of the church. I distinctly remember thinking how odd it was that the room was so ordinary, and Jesus was missing from the cross. Where was he? I wondered.

I remember actually leaning over and asking the person sitting next to me where Jesus was. Why wasn't he on the cross? The simple answer I received then would, in this moment, years later, change everything.

"He is here – with us."

Their response was not meant to be a theological commentary as to whether or not we should have crucifixes with Jesus on them hanging in our churches, don't let your mind go there. They thought they were being clever and probably a bit funny. I let the moment pass without another thought. Until that catalytic moment, somewhere between falling from the sky and hitting the ground.

"He is here – with us."

Why would he be here with me, let alone willing to help me? So many things had changed since that day. I spent enough time in that church to learn that I truly had a need for a Savior, there was no denying that fact. God was offering me the gift of salvation, which meant spending eternity with Him, but I walked away. I failed Him. I did all the things I knew not to do, and none of the things I was supposed to. I chose to let anger, pride, and rejection drive my decisions, and I chased fun and worldly pleasure all the way to this falling airplane.

I was immediately overcome with guilt, and shame fought to keep me from believing that God would still be interested in me, in spite of everything that had transpired between us. But somehow, purely by His grace, I dared to believe it.

"He is here – with me."

God had not given up His pursuit of me, even after everything I had done to mess things up. This realization gave me the courage to pray, which was something I hadn't done in a very long time. Actually, it was more like a bargain than a prayer. "Jesus, I promise if you save me, I will clean up my act. I will stop living with my boyfriend and give up my life of crime. I will be a good mom and go back to church..." and on and on.

At first, it was a frantic, one-sided conversation, but at some point, the most glorious thing happened: I caught a true glimpse of my life, in light of Jesus. It all suddenly made sense. This was an issue of my eternal soul, and though I had done nothing to deserve it, God's offer of heaven was still standing. He had not changed His mind about me. At that moment, I realized what I needed most was an eternal destination shift.

The bargaining was over. Tears streamed down my face as I cried out loud, "I am not asking you to save my life. If I have to die in this plane, all that matters to me, right now, is that I want to be with you."

Everyone must make a decision about their eternity. To not make a decision, or to decide you don't believe in an afterlife, is still a decision. I am forever thankful for the friends I had in the past who loved me enough to tell me the truth about Jesus and who pressed me to make a decision about my eternity, even though I acted as if I wasn't listening. I am especially thankful for those five words, "He is here - with us."

...so is my word that goes out from my mouth: It will not return to me empty, but will accomplish what I desire and achieve the purpose for which I sent it. (Isaiah 55:11 NIV)

That truth was planted deep in my heart, and when the moment was right, it accomplished everything it was sent to do. I am still amazed at how God was so very patient with my process, even though I chose to wait until what felt like the very last moment of my life. I have never been so certain of anything. Though it sounds absolutely crazy, there in that plane, falling from the sky, pilots screaming at one another, storm raging, darkness enveloping the cabin, my soul was at peace and joy began to rise up in my spirit. It was unstoppable.

I started to sing. Yes, I did. My hands were lifted in the air, and I was smiling from ear to ear, belting out some mismatched lines from the few worship songs I had learned in my brief time at that little church. I couldn't help myself. I was singing with every ounce of strength I had. It doesn't make any sense that joy and peace could exist in such a messed-up moment, but I am now fully convinced that they can.

Obviously at the time, the pilots failed to understand what was going on and were not at all happy with me. The South American pilot kept screaming at me to "shut the f*** up." The expletives and threats spewing from his mouth faded into the background, and nothing could stop me.

We were falling from the sky, and all I could do was praise.

Suddenly, in the midst of what seemed like complete beautiful chaos, pilot's screaming, storm raging, praise songs belting, I heard God's voice. It wasn't an audible sound, but an inner voice so strong and clear, it was undeniable. "When the plane hits you, hit it back. Hold on Julie. Fight back." Something inside me grabbed on to the slightest hope that I could survive, and it caused me to spring into action.

Faith was ignited, and I dared to believe the next impossible thing.

My thinking became crystal clear, and I knew exactly what to do. I looked around the plane and grabbed some jackets, put them on my lap, tightened my seatbelt, bent over, and grabbed the front of my chair. I placed my feet on the rear-facing seat in front of me and braced myself for impact. When the plane hit me, I was ready to hit it back.

We crashed.

Even now, after all these years have passed, I am still overcome with emotion realizing that the person in this story is me. I made those decisions, cried those tears, and lived through the pain of that very messed-up life. Time and truth have since helped me to make sense of it all and come to a place where I am able to clearly see the powerful lessons of mercy, love, and redemption woven in and through the difficulty. I am in awe of his unrelenting love. I am struck by His insistence that all men come to the knowledge of Him. I am blown away by his persistence and His refusal that anyone should perish. But this is all to His glory.

Of course, there is more to the story, and we will get to that. On our journey together, I will share what it means to recalculate the direction of your life and find your way forward. We will discuss mental agreements that have made a mess of your thinking and you will learn what it means to reclaim your God-inspired destiny. And of course, we will most certainly address how to deal with all of those other messy people in your life.

Right now, your life might feel as if it is spiraling out of control, and you are bracing yourself for a crash landing that you are sure you can't survive. Or you could be watching your dreams slip away in the midst of seemingly uncontrollable circumstances. I get it. As uncomfortable as it is, I want to encourage you to let this moment be the catalyst for real and lasting change.

Let's begin. I want you to do two things:

1. Believe Him.

God has not changed His mind about you. Resist the voices in your brain that tell you there is no way out and that your mistakes have made a mess of your life for good. I promise you that He has perfect visibility of all that is happening, or not happening, in your life right now. He is not surprised to find you exactly where you are, even if that place is in a plane falling from the sky. Dare to believe He is here-with you and, He has a plan to help you find your way forward.

2. Change your destination.

Everyone will make a decision about their eternity. To not make one is still a decision. You must settle the issue of your soul. If heaven is your preferred destination, will you put your faith in the finished work of Jesus Christ, who gave His life so that you could get there? I pray that you do.

Your present circumstances don't determine where you can go; they merely determine where you start.
—Nido Qubein

Chapter 2

STARTING POINT

STARTING POINT
"What are you doing here?"

The process of finding your way forward will require you to step outside of your comfort zone. You will need to be committed, and you will need to be brave, but before you begin, you will need to be honest. A truthful assessment of where you are right now is vital to recalculating the direction of a life gone rogue.

In this day and age, we have come to rely heavily on portable navigation systems, otherwise known as a GPS. We have these in our cars and on our phones, and they faithfully – and sometimes, rather annoyingly – remind us of the direction we should be traveling if we want to reach our desired destination. I don't know how I ever find my way anywhere without one. The truth is, even with modern technology, I can sometimes still manage to get lost. If my GPS had a voice of its own, I swear it would say things like:

"What part of turn left did you not understand?"

"Really? That was what you thought I said?"

"How's that working for you?"

"Let me know when you are ready to listen."

Receiving direction from others is not one of my strong suits therefore, I was not surprised to find that input was number 34 out of 34 strengths on my *Strengthfinders* personality test. Even as a child, I would do anything possible to work problems out on my own rather than ask for help. Help is just another form of input. Apparently, I don't like input. I now understand this was one of the factors that kept me from ever moving forward out of the mess I was in. I simply could not or would not admit that I was lost.

In order to be of any help, a good GPS will always begin by asking, "Can I use your current location?" Yes, you have to be honest about where you are. You can't deny it, and you can't avoid it. If you want to begin moving forward in the right direction, you must first be able to admit where you are. In order to begin finding my way forward, I had to stop hiding and be honest about the mess I was in. This proved to be much harder than it sounds.

As the plane was falling out of the sky, I had what I like to call an eternal destination shift. The trajectory of my life completely changed when I decided the place where I wanted to be at the end of my life here on earth, was with God. I accepted His gift of eternal life through Jesus and that settled the question in my mind about what was next if I died. My heart was at peace with that. The next logical question remained.

"What's next if I live?"

We broke through the clouds and began violently hitting the tops of the trees in the wetlands surrounding the airport. I remember the sound of it so clearly. It was thunderingly loud. The plane was pitching back and forth, and I could feel the side walls pressing against me. As I braced myself for impact, I found strength in the words I repeated, "When the plane hits you, hit it back. "When the plane hits you, hit it back."

The aircraft slammed into the ground and came to a screeching halt. The cabin was silent and dark, and for a split second, I wondered if I was even alive. My foot was stuck between the seat in front of me and what I thought was the sidewall of the plane. I couldn't get it free. In the smoky darkness, I could sense someone approach and heard them shout, "Move." My foot was pulled out of my shoe, and my seat belt was unbuckled. Someone picked me up and the next thing I remember, I was out on the wing of the plane. Once more, I heard a shout, "Move!" I slid down the wing and ran as fast as I could to a cover of trees a short distance away.

I could see that one of the pilots was badly injured, and the other, was attempting to get him out of the cockpit and carry him to safety. I realized there was no possible way that either of them could have been the one who helped me get out of the plane, and I struggled to make sense of what had just happened. As I stood there, shocked and confused, with my one, bare foot sinking into the mud, the plane burst into flames.

The small church nestled in the community that was hidden in the swamp land surrounding the crash site was having their weeknight service. A young boy who had snuck out to play saw the plane go down and notified the church people, who immediately set out to see what happened. When they found us, I was still in shock and strangely preoccupied with my missing shoe, my bare foot, and the muddy ground.

Unable to focus on anything else, I was frozen in place, and I could not take even one small step forward. I knew I had to move. I wanted to get as far away from that place as I could, but I just couldn't seem to put one foot in front of the other. Realizing I was never going to be able to walk out on my own, one of the men eventually picked me up and carried me over his shoulder out of the swamp.

I was taken to the home of one of the church ladies and laid on her couch. She was very old, and there was an authority to the way she carried herself. She caught my eye as she approached and began shaking her head back and forth as she asked me one, heart-piercing question.

"Baby, what are you doing here?"

There was a slight sadness in her voice. I had no idea how to answer her. How could I tell her how messy my life had become? Up to that moment, I don't think I had ever allowed myself to evaluate my life and decisions through the lens of truth. Honesty would have required me to change, and the fear of change was worse than being trapped in a life that I hated.

"You know you don't belong here," she said, but this time, she smiled. She sat beside me stroking my hair and started to pray. I couldn't hold back the tears. Her words were positive and encouraging, and the sound of her voice comforted me and made me feel safe. That was not something I had felt in a long time.

> "The Sovereign LORD has given me a well-instructed
> tongue, to know the word that sustains the weary."
> (Isaiah 50:4 NIV)

The people living in the area surrounding the swamplands were very poor. They had no addresses and lived with very few modern conveniences. This made things very difficult for the rescue teams that were dispatched when the plane went down. I was thankful for the extra time it took to find us because leaving that peace-filled home meant stepping back into the chaos of my life.

When the ambulances and paramedics finally arrived on the scene, I was immediately strapped to a gurney and quickly removed from the house. Real life descended upon me like a whirlwind.

There were a million questions from multiple people. What's my name? Do I have pain anywhere? Do I have medical insurance? Was there anyone else on the plane? Can I recall the details of the crash? Where were we going? Who is my emergency contact? Have I been drinking or taking drugs? Am I pregnant? They were all simple questions that should have been easily answered, unless you are living a life that is a total lie.

Messy people do not like questions.

Even the simplest questions press on the truth, and that is not something that we are prepared to deal with. Honesty requires an active response, and that can be more terrifying than living a lie. But, sometimes, you just have to say it... out loud. You have to admit what just happened, or where you find yourself, or how you are doing. Messy things left hidden and in silence have great potential to grow into giant roadblocks in your life. They will keep you stuck in a destructive holding pattern and prevent you from moving forward.

When the emergency room doctor examined me, he could not believe I had just survived a plane crash. I had no broken bones. No concussion. No cuts that required stitches. Outside of expecting some heavy bruising, he could find absolutely nothing wrong with me. I was lucky, he said, but I knew luck had nothing to do with it. I was a miracle.

The South American pilot was the only one who had sustained serious injuries, and I have no idea if he lived or died. As is the case in the dark world of trafficking, I would never see him again. Because of the connections and the relationship between my ex and the authorities he cooperated with, there would be no more questions asked.

Within a few hours of arriving at the hospital, I walked out in bare feet, holding my one shoe and mulling over the one simple question I was asked by the old woman: "What are you doing here?"

Making the call to my mom that night was painful. I had learned to be a master at hiding all of the messy parts of my life, but something had changed in me and as difficult as it seemed to admit my failure, I knew that I needed to tell her what had happened and let the pieces fall where they may. When I heard her voice, I struggled to hold back the tears. It was the first time I would say the words out loud.

"I crashed. It wasn't that bad. (lie) I am fine. (lie) Can you pick me up at the airport? I want to come home."

She had very few questions, and I was relieved, because at the time, I had very few answers that made any kind of sense. She simply said to let her know the time I would arrive, and she would be there – nothing more. The tone of her voice was a mixture of anger, worry, and hopeless exasperation. I was breaking her heart, and I knew it. What I didn't know at the time was how I was going to fix it.

The next morning, I went back to the crash site to see if any of my things had survived the fire, most importantly my shoe. I had no idea why, but there was something significant about that shoe. Several investigators were wandering around the wreckage attempting to complete their reports about the incident. I approached one and told him I had been a passenger on the plane. He asked me where I had been sitting. "Left side, passenger," I replied.

His response will be etched in my memory forever: "Lady,

all I have to say is that it would be a miracle if you were sitting in that seat, because that seat is no longer there." He walked me over to the plane, pointed to a tree wedged into the place where my seat used to be and said, "Nobody could have survived that."

I just stood, staring in complete disbelief, until something caught my eye. Stuck between the tree and the wreckage of the plane was my other shoe. It was right where I said it would be and it proved beyond a shadow of a doubt that my survival was an absolute miracle. I walked over and dislodged it, showed it to the very confused investigator, and walked away.

This is where the movie usually ends, right? Lesson learned. She lives happily ever after. Or jump to six months later and see how everything works out perfectly, and she is living the life she had always dreamed about. That would have been so nice.

Life is not a movie, and we have to live out the moments between the scenes.

This was only the beginning for me. I could not have known that the fight to free myself from the wreckage of my life would be almost as dangerous as falling from the sky in an airplane. Still, the fact that I was alive was proof that God must have cared enough about me to intervene in impossible, even miraculous ways.

If God believed my life was worth saving, I wanted to know why.

Why did it matter to God if I lived or died? In light of the fact that we both knew I had settled the issue of eternity, was there still significance in my life here on earth? Seeing my shoe lodged in the wreckage caused the reality of what just happened to come crashing down upon my heart and sent my thoughts into overdrive. I had so many unanswered questions. How did I live through a crash that should have killed me? Who helped get me out of the plane? Was that an angel? Do I believe in angels? What's next?

At the time, the answer to all of these was a resounding, "I don't know." These were questions I knew only God could answer. There was however, one question I knew I had to address if I was going to find my way forward out of this mess.

"Baby, what are you doing here?"

I had been living with a broken internal GPS, running in circles, lost, and getting nowhere fast. It was time for a major life recalculation. Now that my destination was clear, I had to be willing to be honest about where HERE was and, to admit the things I had done that got me HERE in the first place.

You have to admit where you are, if you want to get to where you are going.

Being willing to admit failure was a critical starting point for me. The Bible calls this process confession. It is the act of acknowledgement of a sinful behavior with an intent to change. Sin, by its Hebrew definition is simply missing the mark. We are instructed to confess or admit the areas where we have missed the mark to

God and to one another. This doesn't mean that we need to walk around constantly berating ourselves and announcing our failures to anyone who is brave enough to listen. Please, don't do that. It is also not taking the blame for everything that has ever gone wrong. Let's face it: not everything is your fault. Yes, it is okay to say that.

Let's leave others to deal with their own stuff. If we continually focus on the faults of others, we will never be able to honestly assess our own. I would guess that there are people in your life who seriously need to change. Messy people often attract each other. Their life might even be all tangled up in your mess, but confession has to be all about you.

The only truth you can own is yours.

It's not going to be easy. Sincere confession does not allow room for deflection or denial. I was a master at both, so I know how difficult it can be to let those things go in pursuit of truth. This might be new territory for you and new can be frightening. Let me encourage you to fight through the fear of it. There is a great reward waiting for you if you will. It might surprise you.

Finally, I confessed all my sins to you and stopped trying to hide my guilt. I said to myself, "I will confess my rebellion to the LORD." And you forgave me. All my guilt is gone.
(Psalm 32:5 NLT)

Yes, here is the beautiful truth. Confession opens the doors of opportunity for us to experience first-hand the mercy and forgiveness that Jesus freely provides. In my case, every point of honesty, every confession, every moment of transparency provided one more glimpse of God's mind-blowing grace in my life. I thought the launching point for my recalculated journey would be my failure and my sin, instead it became His grace, His mercy and His love.

So, the answer to the question, "Baby, what are you doing here?" was this: I Messed up. God's response to my answer was, "My Son has already taken care of it. Now we need to move because just as the old woman said, "You know you don't belong here."

God is not surprised to find you right where you are, even if where you are is a gigantic messy swamp of your own making. In fact, He sees not only the way out, but the way forward to a life that was inspired for you before you had the ability to make even one bad decision. He knows what's next and it is more than you can ask or imagine. So, let's deal with where you are right now. Let's get real. Let's be honest.

I want you to do three things:

1. Admit where you are.

It's time to admit that you feel lost, or broken, or that you are living in the center of one great big mess. Don't be afraid to be honest with God. He already knows what your deal is, and condemnation is not His thing.

2. Seek truth.

You must have truth as your launching point. The Bible tells us the role of the Holy Spirit is to reveal God's thoughts to us, so ask Him and open your heart to what He wants to show you. Let Him remove the blinders of denial, deception, and dishonesty from your eyes so you can see your situation with clarity.

3. Confess and receive.

Spend some time in confession to God. Say it out loud. As you do, you will be able to experience His grace and forgiveness. This will change the game for you and is an essential launching point for recalculating the direction of your life. Next, find a trustworthy person and be honest about your mess. Make sure this is someone who will empathize with your pain but insist that you focus on your progress. Keep this conversation about you. One more time – keep it about you. If you find yourself complaining about someone else, stop saying words.

Start by doing what's necessary; then do the possible;
suddenly you will be doing the impossible.
— *Francis of Assisi*

Chapter 3

BREAK IT DOWN

BREAK IT DOWN

You have to move.

Staying where you are is not an option. Retreat might bring a temporary reprieve, but it won't help to clean things up or get your life moving in the right direction.

The mess can be daunting. You could be in a marriage that feels broken beyond repair, or maybe you are facing a mountain of debt that will take years to pay off. Perhaps it is an addiction problem – like drugs, porn, food, or gambling – which can often feel like giant, insurmountable roadblocks in your life. If you allow yourself to dwell too much on the impossibilities, you will, most likely, never find the motivation to begin.

You could fail.

The thought of that might be more than you can bear. Nobody wants to embrace situations that have the potential for disappointment or pain. Chances are that you have failed before and lived to talk about it which means you are stronger than you think you are. The bottom line is, at some point, you must decide if staying where you are is worse than facing the possibility of failing one more time.

Don't interpret your future through the lens of your past.

You might believe that you don't have what it takes to face the uncertainties of the future. History may even validate that this is true, but God's grace can be a game-changer. It is always sufficient and perfectly timed. Grace will never fail you, and it will be there to carry you through exactly when you need it. It won't be a moment too soon, and it won't be a moment too late.

You have what you need today, and God has already provided for your tomorrow so don't make decisions about tomorrow's challenges with today's grace. Take the step and trust Him to fill in the gaps where you fall short. Until you do, you will not know how strong you can be, how resilient, or how much you can handle.

Every journey, no matter how long, has to begin with one first step.

Life coach and motivational speaker Tony Robbins shares a strategy he developed when tasked with improving the marksmanship of U.S. soldiers. Having no previous experience with firing a gun, he consulted several experts and learned a very simple, but powerful, training technique.

Bring the target closer.

Rather than keeping the targets at a distance, where the soldiers were repeatedly going to fail, he brought the targets in close enough to ensure that everyone could succeed. Building on that small victory, he was then able to move the targets back in small increments and eventually improve their overall accuracy by 50 percent. It is amazing how small, incremental victories add up to giant accomplishments.

You can always do one small thing. And one small thing is progress.

Just like those soldiers, I had to learn what it meant to bring the target closer. I could see nothing but giant roadblocks in the path that lay ahead of me and yet, I knew I needed to move. There was no other choice. I had to find a way to take at least one small step forward because staying put was not an option for me anymore.

It would take two planes to get home. The first departed from the airport, where we were trying to land when we crashed. The flight would be on a small plane, slightly bigger than the one I had just left in pieces on the ground. The trauma of literally falling out of the sky less than 48 hours earlier and the thought of flying again made me physically ill. All I knew was that I desperately needed to get home to my son and to have him close. I had no idea what the future held for us, but I knew if I allowed myself to think too far ahead, the fear of it would paralyze me.

I couldn't conceive of ever getting on another airplane again, but I could get in a cab – so, I did. I took a step, allowed myself that victory, and then, decided to do the next small thing that moved me in the direction of home.

Just do the next thing.

Take a cab.

Get to the airport.

Buy a ticket.

Board the plane. That was hard.

Sit down and put my seatbelt on.

I cried the whole way to Miami, disembarked from the small plane, and threw up on the tarmac. The next flight would have me trapped on the plane for five times longer than the last one. I forced myself to stay in the moment and committed to myself that I would just keep taking the next small step until I couldn't.

Walk back into the airport.

Buy another ticket.

Go through security.

Find the gate.

Wait... one more minute, one more time.

Board the plane. That was hard.

Find my seat.

Sit down and put my seatbelt on.

These things all seem like pretty easy tasks on the scale of life, but they were monumental accomplishments for someone who had just fallen out of the sky. Every step was a small victory that brought me closer to home.

> *"Do not despise these small beginnings, for the Lord*
> *rejoices to see the work begin..."*
> *(Zechariah 4:10 NLT)*

Thinking back to that time, I find it funny that during the whole flight, it never occurred to me that I could pray for things that seemed so small and insignificant like finding my gate or waiting one more minute. Obviously, I still had a few things to learn about how God wanted to work in my life. He and I had worked out the grand issues of my eternity, but I assumed it was completely my responsibility to work out the mess of my life.

Assuming what God will or will not do based upon our limited knowledge of His character will limit His ability to help.

I would like to say that I arrived home, got my act together, and never looked back. Lesson learned? Not exactly. Some lives, especially those that are connected to criminal activity, are not so easy to walk away from so simply saying my goodbyes and walking out the door to a better life was not an option. My ex would have never let me go without a fight and when I say fight, I literally mean fight. The flight home gave me ample opportunity to consider the fact that I had very few options. Go back to living with the ex or try to leave. Both were dangerous. Despite the fact that I had just taken some courageous steps in the right direction, I made a decision to choose the path of least resistance and took a self-imposed detour that took me completely off course.

I will never forget the look on my mom's face as I limped out of the airport. The bruising I had over half of my body made it painful to walk. This, combined with my ragged clothes – which I had not changed since the crash – and puffy eyes from the lack of sleep and non-stop crying made for a dismal scene. I was so ashamed.

Her expression was blank, but I knew she was angry. Without saying a word, she simply turned and walked away. Who could blame her? My life was clearly out of control. I was putting myself and my son, her grandson, in harm's way. She had no idea how to stop it. Sadly, neither did I. Looking back now, with a healthy lens and being a mom and a grandma myself, I believe I should thank my mom every day for not strangling me on the spot.

By the way, thanks Mom.

I should have been honest with her and asked for help, but that would have required me to have answers I didn't have and to make decisions that I was still unable— or unwilling—to make. I hated that this made me feel so powerless and foolish, so I did what I always did when faced with feelings I had no ability to cope with, I let anger take over and I chose to be mad...at her.

Misplaced anger is a toxic coping mechanism that will drive you further into isolation.

Anger had functioned as a toxic or unhealthy coping mechanism in my life for a very long time. I used it to protect my heart from emotions I didn't want to deal with or from people who seemed unsafe. If someone hurt me, I would respond by being angry at them. As long as I was angry, I wouldn't let them close, and if they couldn't get close, they could no longer hurt me. In this case, my mother's disappointment in me pressed on the truth of my failure. It hurt me to think that I had let her down and caused her so much pain. I was unable to cope with those emotions in a healthy way, so anger stepped in and ran interference. If I am angry with you, you cannot get close enough to show me that I failed you. I don't have to face it, feel it, or deal with it.

One important thing to understand is that the next small step may not always be a physical action. You might need to begin on the inside. It could be a mind shift, an attitude adjustment or a letting go of something that you've held for way too long. You can choose to be kind. Forgive. Trust. Let someone off the hook. Cease to be angry.

The next thing I needed to do after disembarking from the plane was to trust. I needed to trust my mom enough to ask for help. That would have meant telling her how bad things actually were behind the scenes of my life. To trust her with that truth meant I had to give her the space and time to work through her fear and disappointment without being offended. It was the next small step that I couldn't take so I turned and went the other way.

With anger firmly in place, I stubbornly determined in my heart that I didn't need help from anyone. I would clean this mess up by myself, and then, I would make things right with the world...and my mom.

Having no other plan in place besides *I messed it up and now I need to fix it*, I picked up Josh and returned to the home where I lived with the drug-addicted, violent ex. One small step forward, two giant steps back. Can't you just hear that internal GPS screaming, "Return to the route."

It's messed-up thinking for sure, but progress can be slow and feel a bit schizophrenic sometimes. Don't be surprised, and don't let this discourage you. Things like toxic coping mechanisms, failure to trust, and faulty mental agreements which we will discuss in the following chapters do not disappear overnight.

Each small step required me to think differently and to consequently acknowledge the fact that, based on past decisions and reactions, I might not have the clearest judgement. This was hard to admit, and it took some practice, but rather than immediately acting on my own instincts, I had to learn to wait for God's direction and trust His lead, even when it made no sense.

Finding your way forward is a marathon not a sprint.

It would not be the last detour for me. The mess in my life was complex and forward progress, at times, was painstakingly slow but small victories will add up to great accomplishments if you don't quit. One thing I have learned about myself through this whole process is, I am not a quitter. If you are taking the time to read this, I would guess that you are not either.

Your mess probably feels like an insurmountable roadblock that you cannot scale. You might even be on a detour right now. Please resist the urge to define your progress by every bad turn. I am confident, you will return to the route if you stay in the game, refuse to quit and turn your attention back to God.

Here are two things that can definitely help:

1. Take the next small step.

You might not be able to leave an abusive situation, find a million dollars that can pay off all your debt, or forgive your husband for every hurt he has caused you. Take a moment and consider what you can do. There is always some small something. If you can't see it, ask God to show you. Take the next small step, and then, take the next one.

2. Celebrate small victories.

We tend to define our lives by the things that are broken, so taking opportunities to celebrate small wins can make a huge difference and create much-needed momentum. This affirmation will also help to build a healthy foundation of success, so when things don't go as planned, you have a competing voice reminding you that all is not lost.

"The best way to find out if you can trust somebody
is to trust them."
— Ernest Hemingway

Chapter 4

THE POWER
OF TRUST

THE POWER OF TRUST
Someone has to know.

Is there someone in your life who you trust enough to help you? Does anyone else know what you are telling me? These are two questions I will typically ask when sitting down with a person who is dealing with a messed-up situation. Often times, the answer is a resounding, almost panic stricken, "NO! Nobody can know. That would make things so much worse. People complicate things."

Two are better off than one for they can help each other
succeed. If one person falls, the other can reach out and help.
But someone who falls alone is in real trouble.
(Ecclesiastes 4:9-10 NLT)

The catalyst for isolation is trust. This can be physical; "I cannot have people in my life because they will find out the truth." Or, it can be purely emotional. "I have many people in my life, but nobody can know what is really going on." It can be self-imposed, meaning you do this to yourself. Or it can be imposed upon you by a victimizer who uses threats of violence, blackmail or harm to keep you from seeking the help you need to get free. This is often the case with people in dangerously abusive situations.

Any way you slice it, isolation is a toxic coping mechanism, which supports denial, creates unhealthy co-dependency and will almost always stall your progress. An isolated life is the perfect place to hide broken things and left hidden, these have a propensity to grow more powerful than you could have ever imagined.

One of the challenges of living in isolation is that you inadvertently trap yourself into a toxic information loop which will greatly limit your ability to see your situation from any other viewpoint but your own or worse, from the other messy people involved in the problem. Insisting upon finding the solution to your mess based solely upon your limited, ground-zero viewpoint might not be the best idea. You need healthy people in your life who are not mired in the practical and emotional details to help you see beyond the dead-end you feel stuck in. Very much like your GPS, they can offer a satellite perspective of your situation and in many cases show you that you indeed have options.

Someone needs to know what's going on and have the freedom to speak, or what might even be more frightening, intervene in your situation. The challenge with this is that you will have to take down the protective walls you have built around you and trust someone enough to tell them the truth.

Trust requires vulnerability.

Webster defines vulnerability as; *putting yourself in a position where you are capable of being physically or emotionally wounded.*

Nothing about that sounds appealing to a person who is doing their best to protect themselves from pain. Vulnerability means that you must come out of hiding and get real with people. It requires you to share the what of what's going on: I am drinking too much. I can't stop looking at porn. My spending is out of control. I am using again. We fight every day. I can't get of bed in the morning. He is violent.

Brene Brown, author of the book *Rising Strong* is a current expert in this area and has a great perspective on vulnerability.

"Vulnerability is not winning or losing; it's having the courage to show up and be seen when we have no control over the outcome. Vulnerability is not weakness; it's our greatest measure of courage."
— *Brene Brown*

Even for the healthiest of people, vulnerability is frightening, but trust is built when you find the courage to open up your life to someone and give them a chance to prove that they will come through for you. When they do, you grow more confident in the relationship and more importantly, you grow more confident in your worth as a person as they now have an opportunity to show you that you are worth their time and attention.

I had more than a few trust issues to overcome.

Nothing in my history supported the practice of allowing people access to my heart in a way that could end up with me being hurt. Believing that the world was a dangerous place, and that people did not have my best interest in mind kept me safe. For me, it was not necessarily in a physical sense. I was careless and abusive with my life, but I always held my emotional cards close. I will give you my body, but never my heart. This was the very broken boundary line of my life, the lie I told myself that I believed would help to keep me safe and in control.

I had so many excuses for my isolation.

I was afraid people would judge me and I honestly believed I deserved it. I would have. I was afraid they would call the police, or tell people, and people complicate things. If I am honest however, the one excuse that dominated all the others was that I was afraid of losing control of the situation. Losing control, was dangerous. One thing I fully trusted was that my ex would make my life a living hell if I ever told.

The choice to return to my home and stay wasn't smart, or healthy, or productive, or sane. It was familiar. Familiarity can often be mistaken for safety. I understood what it took to survive in that situation, and I trusted in my ability to manage the chaos and keep Joshua and I safe.

Familiarity is a false comfort that defies change.

Leaving was unfamiliar territory, and I had no plan for that. Staying in my comfort zone no matter how broken and convoluted that idea was, at least kept me dependent upon the only person I had determined I could really trust…ME.

I kept the plane crash a secret from everyone. I hid the bruises, and true to form, kept all my conversations superficial, so there would be no questions asked. It looked like business as usual on the outside, but something had really changed and not for the better. The 'Ex' returned home in a mental state that seemed to be darker and more dangerous than ever. I found it almost impossible to cope with the manic behavior brought about by his growing cocaine addiction. It was very apparent to me that staying was becoming way too dangerous, but with my limited perspective, I could see no way out.

I had hit a dead-end, with no apparent options.

Fear of reprisal and physical harm paralyzed me and kept me from considering any next steps forward. The plane crash hadn't killed me, but if I tried to leave, I fully believed my ex would. His drug dependence and mental state continued to grow increasingly more dangerous, and I took his threats of harm seriously. Besides this, I had no idea how I would survive. I had no money saved, my credit card was maxed out, and I had pretty much isolated myself from everyone who might have been willing to help me.

I did, however, have a job. I worked as a fitness instructor at a high-end athletic club, where wealthier clientele would come to exercise, socialize, and meet for drinks. Several times a week,

I taught a 5:00 p.m. fitness class in a racquetball court in front of the bar. The pastor of a local church in the neighborhood was a member and would often walk by, saying hello as he passed. Pastor Zac knew just about everyone by name, and everyone seemed to love him. Occasionally, he would stop by my class, and ask when he would see me at church. I would usually just laugh and make some sarcastic remark under my breath, like asking if hell had frozen over yet. I had no idea how he knew my name.

There was a part of me that questioned why he would want me in his church. Everyone at the club knew that I was not church material. I never hid the fact that I was living with a man who was not my husband. I almost always had a hangover and had very little regard for my reputation. Besides, what kind of a pastor hung out in a gym, with a bar, and a whole mess of sinners? He clearly had no regard for his reputation either. He didn't fit in any of my religious, Christian, church person boxes and that made him both dangerous and interesting to me.

Most of my energy since the accident had been consumed with surviving day to day, but there were moments when I could feel the pull on my heart to seek understanding of it. I started to wonder if I might be able to trust this guy enough to help me figure out what exactly had happened in that plane and what it all meant in my life. Everything seemed to have changed for me, but I could not figure out exactly why or what I was supposed to do with it all. I considered that based upon his relentless invitations to come to church, he might not be put off by my less that sparkling reputation. My past experiences with church people did not line up at all with that kind of thinking, and Pastor Zac was a church person. My agreement in that plane was with God and God alone. I was not interested in dealing with church people and based upon my history with them, I had determined that they were not interested in dealing with me.

Growing up Mexican seemed to be synonymous with growing up Catholic. I know that is not true, but as I child I never knew there were any other options. We went to church because that is what we did. It was a practice that was embedded in our culture. In our family, we never prayed or spoke of faith or God at home, we just went to church. I suppose everyone just assumed we would figure it all out if we were there enough. Now, as an adult, I have grown to appreciate and understand the great value of approaching a Holy God with humility and great reverence, but in the absence of any other voices in my life that validated the loving and grace-filled character of God, I simply grabbed a hold of the obey or be judged parts and ran with it. This is in no way a knock on the Catholic denomination. It is more a commentary about how easily children, left to their own interpretation of religious practices, and without loving connected people to help them develop balanced and healthy perspectives of God, can get it very wrong.

I am not even sure how we were able to afford it, but my sister and I were put in Catholic school rather than attend the free public school in our neighborhood. It had to be a big sacrifice for us to attend, and I should have been grateful, but I absolutely hated it. In the first three years of my school career, I spent a great deal of time being reprimanded for my lack of cooperativeness and wet my pants so much my mom had to keep extra clothes for me in the nurse's office. Nobody thought to question why, they just solved the problem of getting me back to class in clothes that did not smell like pee.

Attending church during the school week was part of our education. Part of that included going to confession. I distinctly remember making up sins to confess because I would get so anxious, I honestly couldn't think of what to say. Who lies to a priest and confesses sins they didn't even commit? Here is a confession from 7-year-old me. I never actually said the prayers they gave me to say as the penance for my made-up sins, I just waited until the person who went in before me was done with their praying and then waited a few minutes more before leaving, just so that the nuns would believe I had actually done it. Oh, and since I am being vulnerable and telling the whole truth, I was the kid that peed in the confessional and didn't tell anyone. I was convinced I was going to hell for that one.

During high school, I had had a few Christian friends, one of whom had a mom who would open her home to anyone who wanted to hang out. Clarice would stand behind the counter in her kitchen and listen to our endless, teenage discussions, and when the moments were appropriate, share about God and her love for Jesus. There was something very different about her faith, and I was always drawn to her. She had a perspective about God that I had never heard before. Years later when my life fell apart and my husband walked out the door, leaving me with a broken heart and a two-month-old baby, that was the first place I ran.

They took me to church. This was the place I described in the first chapter of the book. The one with the empty cross. I was willing to try anything that had the potential to ease the pain and rejection I was feeling from my broken marriage, so at the first opportunity, I acknowledged my need for a savior and prayed to accept Jesus into my life. Based upon my limited perception of God, I was quick to agree that I was deserving of hell. I was convinced that if Jesus didn't save me, I would be in big trouble, but I understood little of His life transforming love. Things did not go smoothly beyond that.

It never dawned on me that my pending divorce was probably not something I should have shared without discretion. I knew I was truly loved and accepted by my friends who brought me to church but the other church people had no idea what to do with the mess of a 19-year-old, emotionally broken, single mom who was going through a divorce. A few of them, who I actually did not know very well, believed the kindest thing to do was to immediately educate me on the theological rules of the church concerning my situation.

I was informed that I would be expected to stay single forever or be reconciled to my husband – who, by the way, was already making plans for marriage number-two. Furthermore, I would be considered an adulteress if I married again, and my new husband would be considered an adulterer and would be disqualified from ever serving in a pastoral or leadership role in the church.

It is not my intent here to criticize their theology. People smarter and more educated than I am have been arguing about this for years. Now, as a pastor myself, I also understand their desire to protect their church from compromise. I have to assume they were probably good, God-fearing people, but they had no relationship with me and therefore, no knowledge of the shame and the guilt I was already carrying from my past. To be fair, nobody did.

It's not the message: it's the method.

The last thing a new convert needs is someone, outside of the context of relationship, leading with the rule book and telling them what their future will be based upon the mistakes of their past. Rules, even the clearly biblical ones, presented in that way to a person who has no fundamental knowledge of God's unconditional love and mercy, create a perfect environment for condemnation. Self-condemnation was something I had grown to be an expert at, so it took off like wildfire in my spirit.

As a baby Christian, who had not yet developed the maturity to process the information in a healthy, balanced way, all I could hear was, "Now that you have accepted Jesus, He will wash away all of your sin. However, the sin of your divorce will never disappear. You will carry that for the rest of your life. It will determine your ability to be a leader in the church or to ever find someone to love you." Based upon my interpretation of their rules, I made a huge assumption.

I had accepted Jesus; I just couldn't believe
He had accepted me.

I was 19, with no plans for the future and a newborn baby. I knew I could never commit to remaining single my whole life. Some would say it was a lack of faith – and I would not disagree – but honestly, the thing that tripped me up the most was pride. I hated to be second at anything and I just couldn't fathom living my life in a community where (in my opinion) I would always be second-rate. There was also no way I would ask someone to compromise their belief system in order to love me. If my husband was never coming back, I had no intention of living single.

Honesty about my situation had opened my life up for review and this felt like rejection. Rejection hurt and with my heart already being so broken, I simply did not have room for the pain of it so I ran as fast and as far away as I could.

My friends tried so hard to keep me connected and to help me understand, but timing is everything and I had a way to go before my heart was ready to receive the kind of love they were offering. The truth is their intervention planted seeds in my heart that would eventually save my life. But none of us would realize that for a very long time.

Because of my less than glorious history and some pretty messy doctrinal assumptions, I never even entertained the idea of going back to church, until Pastor Zac decided to stop by my class and say hello again and again and again. He was persistent if nothing else and everything I sensed about him told me I could trust him. It sounded crazy even to me, but I knew it was time to take one next small step. I simply had to walk into that church.

Letting people close can be difficult and sometimes terrifying but God never intended for you to walk this journey alone. Here are two things you can do that will help you break free from isolation.

1. Trust someone.

It's time to find someone who you can trust and trust them. It might be someone already in your life or someone who has just shown up on the scene, but you can tell they are a solid person with integrity. Sure, there is a great possibility that they will let you down, but you will never know if you don't try. I know you are strong enough to handle that if it happens and even if it does, you will be more convinced than ever that you can do hard things.

2. Dare to be vulnerable.

You will never know if you can trust someone unless you give them a chance to know who you really are. Rejection is a possibility so you will have to be brave. Be smart about it and make sure that the people involved are trustworthy people and when the timing is right, take down those walls and give someone a chance to show up for you.

...Behold, we have left everything and followed you
— Mark 10:28 NASB

Chapter 5

EVEN IF MOMENTS

EVEN IF MOMENTS
You will surrender to something.

There is a story in the Bible about three young men who were facing persecution under a tyrant king who was threatening to burn them alive if they refused to bow to him in the place of God. Their response to the king was, "Our God is able to save us, but EVEN IF He doesn't, we will never bow to you." To make a long story short, they put aside fear, surrendered their future to God, and courageously walked into the fire.

"Even if" moments are the manifestation of true surrender.

They are a declaration of your devotion and your commitment to put all other things aside for the sake of something more valuable. In the case of these three young men, their EVEN IF moment told the world that their hearts would surrender to no one else but God, even if it meant being burned alive.

An "even if" attitude closes the door to the torment of fear.

It was settled. The price for their surrender to God was taken into consideration, and they were willing to pay it. Because of this, even the fear of an excruciating death could have no power over them. The enemy was no longer able to torment them.

I have often sat with people who are seeking counsel about a messy situation in their life that they would like to change. As we dig into the discussion, it is clear that though they may want a resolution to their problem, their lives are fully surrendered to the fear that often accompanies that change.

"I am afraid that…

If I leave, I will be alone again.

If I don't use, I won't make it through the day.

If I let this go, they will think they got away with it.

If I forgive, he will do it again."

The truth is, as long as their lives are surrendered to the fear of what may happen, they might as well get really good at staying where they are.

Prioritizing fear will always hold you hostage in your mess.

It's important to learn that you can reprioritize your emotions. In other words, you can decide what will be the dominant emotion that drives your actions. Once you settle this in your mind, emotions like fear, anger, anxiousness, and worry will have to take a backseat to more life- giving desires – like love for your family and devotion to God. Jesus modeled this perfectly.

> "…Because of the joy awaiting Him, He endured the cross,
> disregarding its shame…"
> (Hebrews 12:2 NLT)

What a great example He set for us as He chose not to consider the shame and the pain of the cross and prioritized the joy of what He was about to do for the entire world. He was joyfully surrendered to the will of His Father. This was the thing he valued above all else and it enabled Him to endure even to the point of death. We can follow in His footsteps. It takes resolve and a lot of practice, but it is an emotional skill worth developing.

Surrendering my life here on earth fully to God was going to take a major reprioritizing of emotions that had driven me in the wrong direction for way too long. The fear of failure, the fear of harm, and the fear of being alone had become the dominant influencers in my life, and these emotions drove the majority of my actions and decisions. The time was coming when I would be given the choice to surrender to something else – or rather, someone else. I had received God's forgiveness and surrendered my eternity to Him but, I still had a lot to learn about His willingness to walk straight into the fire with me.

Every minute of my life was accounted for. My ex literally knew when I walked out the door, where I was going, how long it would take before I returned, and exactly what I was wearing – down to my undergarments. I could see no safe pathway out of the mess, which was precisely the problem. In practical terms, there was no "safe" pathway out.

It was risky, but I managed to sneak away under the guise of teaching a new class at a gym in a different city... Yep... I lied to go to church. Sunday was out of the question, so I decided to show up to a mid-week Bible study. Sitting alone in the back, I cried through the whole study. As usual, I kept to myself, but there was one, relentless young man who noticed I was clearly in need of some help. Despite my less-than- welcoming vibe, he was not afraid to ask who I was and what I was doing there.

Pastor Zac had proven faithful to His word and welcomed me into his Bible study without any qualifying questions. Now, I felt it was time to finally trust someone with the whole truth, and this guy, like Zac seemed pretty sincere. Besides, he wasn't associated with anyone in my life or at my work so I could easily cut him out of my life if he proved to be unsafe. One night after the study, he stopped me to ask how I was doing. I spilled it, every shame-filled, terrifying detail. The words erupted from my spirit and I held nothing back. It felt so good to finally say it out loud. That poor guy. I thought he would run for the hills, but he simply listened compassionately and responded without commentary or advice. "When you are ready to leave, I will help you. In the meantime, I will be your friend." And he was, without judgement, and without further questions or conditions. From that point on, he did not become overly involved in the details of my mess but remained consistent in his friendship offering encouragement and kindness.

When you are ready.

Everything hinged on those four words. Nothing could change until I was ready, and it was smart of him to know that.

Over the course of the next few weeks, I did everything I could not to miss the Bible study. I was so happy to be learning the basics of my very basic faith. The best thing of all was that I was beginning to understand what had actually happened in that plane when I surrendered my eternity to God.

Pastor Zac was able to make the scriptures plain and easy to understand. I secretly set aside money and bought a Bible, kept it hidden, and read it whenever I could find the time. The more I learned about what it meant to be a Christian, the more I discovered that there were still a number of things in my life that had not been fully surrendered to God.

I was well acquainted with surrendering to fear, manipulation, hopelessness, and even anger, jealousy, and lust. But the God kind of surrender was the real deal. It meant every aspect of my life was no longer my own: heart, body, soul, spirit, emotions, thoughts, and will. I wanted this so badly and began praying that God would show me what it meant to live this way and strengthen me to do it.

As my heart began to open to the possibilities of surrendering all to God, an opportunity came that would put my newfound commitment to the test. One day, in a paranoid, jealous rage, the Ex assaulted me – ripped off my clothing and threw me out into the front yard. Violent events like this were not uncommon but this time I could tell things were dangerously out of control. Naked, sobbing, and scared, I managed to climb through a window and sneak into one of the back bedrooms, locking the door. When he realized I was back in the house, he began violently pounding on the door, screaming that he would kill me. I knew that if something didn't change soon, he probably would.

Surrender to the problem or the problem solver. It's your choice.

This was the moment. I had to make a choice between surrendering to fear and the lunatic at the door – which would have been my typical response – or surrendering everything to God and placing my trust fully in Him. I chose God. As the screaming and pounding at the door continued in the background, I knelt by the bed and made one more commitment to God. "I know that I won't survive much longer if something doesn't change. If you would help me get free from this, for the rest of my life, I will serve only you."

It was that simple, and there was no turning back. Whether I had five minutes or fifty years, it was all His. God got everything. The moment I finished praying, the situation turned: the screaming and violence ceased, and he walked away, leaving me alone. For the moment, I was safe, but I knew it was time to leave, EVEN IF it meant my worst fears coming to pass. If I left with only the clothes on my back, I had to trust that God could provide. If he tried to harm me, I had to trust that God could protect me. EVEN IF God chose to do nothing, I was still leaving.

I had surrendered fully to God. I would no longer surrender to anything else.

The fear of what might happen had held me hostage for too long. Once I was able to give up the dread of it, I was free from the power of it. I still had to walk through the fire, but as my Bible study friend had said, I was ready.

My mind was made up and the only thing left to do was... to *do* it. Rather than take matters into my own hands, which is what I would have normally done, I surrendered it to God, and prayed that He would show me my next steps forward.

It didn't take long. Plans had been made for the ex to be out of the house for an entire day leaving me alone at home, which almost never happened. I took the opportunity to sneak away and attend a Sunday night service at church, thinking I could make it back to the house before he got home. When I arrived back home, his car was not in the driveway, and all the lights were out in the house. I assumed he was still away and was grateful that I would not have to concoct some sort of excuse for where I had been, until I walked through the front door and found him sitting in the dark – gun in hand, high, and out of his mind with anger.

He was furious. After a few rounds of screaming jealous accusations and threats, he stood, with gun pointed directly at me, and I braced myself for what was next. To my complete surprise, instead of pulling the trigger, he stood his ground and yelled, "Get the f***out! I had to move. God was opening a door, and it was time to trust Him and step through it. I couldn't believe he was throwing me out. That had never happened before. After one, Academy Award-winning protest just to ensure he believed this was his idea, I calmly walked out the door, got in my car, and left. It would be a few days before he would realize I was never coming back.

I distinctly remember the overwhelming feeling of relief as I drove away. I had no home, not a cent to my name, and only the clothes on my back; peace made absolutely no sense. This was only the beginning of what would turn out to be an excruciatingly long and dangerous process, but God had given me the grace and courage in that moment to take the next step forward. Regardless of what happened next, I knew I was free.

I drove directly to my parent's house, swallowed my pride, and asked them to take me in. I needed help with Josh, and my dad – a former gang member or 'leader of the car club' as he called it – was the only person I trusted enough to stand up to the fight that was surely coming.

My mom and dad graciously agreed to let me move in but made it very clear that they would only provide care for my son, and though I would be allowed to stay, they would not give me any help beyond that. Unlike that day in the airport, I let them express their anger and frustration at the dangerous situation

I had now put us all in. I listened without being defensive and chose humility instead of anger. That night, Joshua and I took up residence in a spare bedroom, and I slept peacefully for the first time in years.

Pride has no place in surrender.

One sign of true repentance is a humble willingness to take responsibility for the pain we have caused others by allowing them the time and space they need to heal, regardless of how long that may take. You can't force people to forgive and forget, and you shouldn't place the responsibility on others to reconcile what you broke. In my case, the process of earning back my parent's trust would take years, but my agreement was with God, alone, and not contingent upon anyone else's buy-in.

Sure, it was tough to face the hurt I had caused my family and to think that none of them really believed that I could truly change. But, EVEN IF nobody ever believed in me, or trusted, or forgave me for what I had done, I knew I was never going back to that mess. I had made a deal with God, and I was keeping my word.

You are surrendered to something. Is it an emotion like fear or anger? Is it a drug or a habit that is destroying you and everyone around you? If you can identify something in your life that is holding you hostage and keeping you from fully surrendering your life to God, maybe it is time for an "EVEN IF" moment.

Here are three steps you can take to start the process:

1. Identify

What is the dominate influencer of your actions right now? Is there a negative emotion that is keeping you stuck in your mess? Ask yourself these questions and identify it. Call it what it is. Say it out loud. If you don't own it, you won't be able to change it.

2. Reprioritize

You know you need to make a move, but you are paralyzed by the fear of what comes next if you do. It is time for an EVEN IF moment. Reprioritize the negative emotions that are influencing your decisions and actions and make them take a back seat to something you value. Trust that God can take care of you, EVEN IF your worst fears come to pass.

3. Surrender

You may have settled the question of your eternity by receiving the gift of forgiveness through Jesus, but have you fully surrendered all of your life to Him? This means everything: your emotions, your thoughts, and your actions? Have you also surrendered the outcomes that will result once you do? Remember, He gave His all for you. Will you give Him back the same?

There is no pit so deep that God is not deeper still.
— Corrie Ten Boom

Chapter 6

LOVE THAT PREVAILS

LOVE THAT PREVAILS
God is a stalker.

Someone once asked me what the title of my book might be. I jokingly answered, "Stalked."

"Because you were stalked by someone who meant you harm?"

"Well, yes, but really because I was stalked by God... in a good way."

God will never stop pursuing us. He will use the good, the bad, and the messy parts of our lives to get our attention, and He will never give up on us.

His love is relentless.

Sometimes, He will allow you to experience what it feels like to sit in your mess for a season if it will bring you to a point where you are ready to move forward. But even in that process, His pursuit of your heart is clear.

Yes, God is a stalker...in the best way possible. Though I couldn't understand it, I grew to accept it. Eventually, I believed it. This is the glory of who He is: His revealed magnificence. A God who loves imperfect people so perfectly, and the one who truly never gives up and never leaves you.

"You have searched me, Lord, and you know me. You know when I sit and when I rise; you perceive my thoughts from

afar. You discern my going out and my lying down; you are
familiar with all my ways. Before a word is on my tongue
you, Lord, know it completely..."
(Psalm 139:1-4 NIV)

You get the picture, right? God is everywhere you are. He knows every detail of your life. There is no escaping His presence. Learning that God was not simply equated with all the dark places in my life, but was present in them, was confusing at first. How could He know everything and not change His mind about me? Why was He so determined? What does it mean that He never leaves me... Never? I had no foundation for understanding this kind of attention or devotion... or maybe, in a really messed-up way, I did.

I was stalked for months without reprieve... and not in a good way.

When the call came, demanding that I return, things got crazy. As expected, the realization that I was not coming home drove my ex into a vicious cycle of rage and depression that lasted almost a year. My life was a full-on, day-by-day, if-God-doesn't-show-up-I-will-not-survive situation.

There was no possibility of getting the authorities involved. He was a drug dealer working with the police as a snitch, turning in smaller scale drug dealers in exchange for immunity. I remember calling one of the detectives who worked for the local police department. After telling him what was going on, he dismissed my complaint, telling me that in fact, I was being investigated for drug trafficking. They were deciding whether to move forward with the case. It was best not to pursue my complaint, he said. Warning received. I never called back.

The custody agreement with Josh's father kept me from leaving town. If I fled, I would have to go alone and leave my baby behind. That was not an option. There was no escaping it, no getting around it. I had to walk through it and deal with the consequences one moment at a time.

For a while, there wasn't a moment of peace. He would wait outside my home and follow me in his car, making sure I knew he was watching my every move. There was no place I could go where he wouldn't follow me and would even show up at church and sit in the row right behind me, whispering threats only I could hear.

"I will hunt you like an animal the rest of your life."

People have asked me why I didn't go to a shelter or call a hotline, but back then, either they did not exist or knowledge of them was limited. Remember, this was the early 80s, home computers were only a vision for the future, and the worldwide web would not be introduced to the public until 1989. Advertisement came in the form of television commercials, the local paper, flyers stapled to telephone poles, and billboards by the side of the road.

If you were in danger and needed help, you had to be home by a phone connected to a wall, or you had to stop at a phone booth. And, you better have a quarter.

Over the next year, I was repeatedly threatened, run off the road with Joshua in the car, taken against my will, and physically assaulted. By God's grace, I managed to escape every single time – sometimes in the most miraculous ways.

And we know that God causes everything to work together for the good of those who love God and are called according to his purpose for them.
(Romans 8:28 NLT)

You would think the continual harassment would have driven me crazy, but it only served to make me stronger and more resolved. It forced me to fully rely on God. I had no other options. I learned that I could turn to Him for even the smallest need and became very acquainted with His continual presence. I was beginning to understand and appreciate the value of God knowing my every move.

Every incident was an opportunity for me to learn something new about the way God wanted to work in my life. It was a time of accelerated growth in my Christian walk like no other I have experienced again. I was able to break my addiction to alcohol and many of the other destructive habits that used to dominate my behavior. The lessons that I learned during that time have served to build a solid foundation of faith that has helped me over the years to encourage others who find themselves facing impossible challenges.

I know God exists.

I believe in miracles.

I have no doubt He will provide.

I am convinced He never leaves us.

I know we can walk through fire with him and not be consumed.

As that year wore on, the situation finally began to shift. I realized, there were a few things I was still holding on to that were inconsistent with what I had learned to be true about God. To begin with, I hated this guy. I was so angry at him and began to hope that one of his many enemies would succeed at finally taking him out of the game for good. Every interaction between us was heated and volatile. We were living in a war zone, and I had to stop it.

If it was true that God had not changed His mind about me, then it had to be true that God had not changed His mind about him. If God could reach down into the pit of darkness that I was living in and rescue me, He could rescue him.

As hard as it would be, I had to allow God to change my heart.

Instead of hanging up over and over again every time he called or screaming into the phone how much I hated him and never wanted to see him again, I began answering the phone and praying for him out loud, thanking God for His life and for how much He loved him. If he was going to call, he was going to have to listen to me pray. The same applied to our face-to-face encounters. If he was going to shove me in a car and drive me around town, threatening to kill me, I was going to sit in the back seat with his friends and pray out loud for their souls, as well. Yep, that happened.

Oddly enough, the second thing that needed to break in me was my attachment to stuff. Yes, the night I left I had walked away from everything I owned, but I realized there was a part of me that was still unwilling to fully let it go. I had taken nothing with me, except a credit card debt of almost $10,000 – which, back in that day, when you only made five dollars an hour, was a lot of money.

For a while, I actually tried to manipulate the situation in hopes of getting my stuff back and possibly convince him to give me the money so I could pay off the debt. It wasn't uncommon for him to have large amounts of cash like that laying around, and I thought if I could make him believe that things could be better between us, he would cooperate and pay off his debt.

This was the hold he had on me: the only reason I was ever willing to entertain a conversation with him, and the thing he held over my head. "If you meet me, I will give you the money." "If you come to the house, I will let you get your stuff back." I actually agreed to meet with him once, hoping that he would follow through with his word. Obviously, it did not go well, and after a violent altercation, I left– empty-handed and condemning myself for having been so stupid.

As I was driving away from that incident, I felt God say to me, "You have to let it go. Release him from the debt and walk away from the stuff that is still holding you hostage." This next step was a tough one. Give up all your stuff.

Fear of loss is powerless when you have given up everything.

When the next call came, saying if I didn't meet with him again, he would dispose of everything I owned, and I would never see another cent, God gave me the grace to respond, "I understand. I don't want my things, and I release you from the debt."

Enraged, he made good on his threat and destroyed everything I owned that was in that house. I kept my word and refused to engage in any more discussions about money. The debt was forgiven. He had no more power over me. I was left with the clothes I was wearing when I walked out the door, my Bible, which was in my car, a few items that were in my locker at the gym where I worked, and some of Joshua's things that were kept at my parent's house.

I can't say it was easy. I can't say I didn't cry real tears at the loss of all the sentimental items like pictures or Joshua's favorite toys. I am willing to admit that losing all the things that had come to define me like expensive clothing, shoes, and jewelry, stung a bit but forced me to see the real value of who I was which was not tied to anything I owned.

Forgiveness was a game changer. Just to clarify, forgiveness didn't mean access, I still had to keep unwavering boundaries to the best of my ability, but my responses were now filtered through the lens of God's love and care. As the year went on, the phone calls subsided, and the continual stalking ceased. For a few years, he would randomly show up somewhere or send me letters or pictures of Josh playing in my parent's front yard just to make sure I knew he was still there, watching me. It was meant to keep me living in fear. What he didn't realize was that God was also still there, watching me, protecting me, providing for me, and most of all, loving me in a way that was completely transforming my life.

This marked the end of this chapter of my life, but it is far from the end of my story. I would never again return to the madness of that season. I still had to deal with the internal reasons I ended up in that plane in the first place, heal from the things that were broken along the way and learn what it meant to live as a committed Christian. It would take commitment and resolve which we will discuss in the next Chapters, but the bottom line was I was free. In more ways than one…I was free.

> *Where can I go from your Spirit?*
> *Where can I flee from your presence?*
> *If I go up to the heavens, you are there;*
> *if I make my bed in the depths, you are there.*
> *If I rise on the wings of the dawn,*
> *if I settle on the far side of the sea,*
> *even there your hand will guide me,*
> *your right hand will hold me fast.*
> *(Psalm 139:7-10 NIV)*

I can still, to this day, barely read the words of this psalm without tears. I know what it feels like to be stalked by someone who means me harm, and I know what it feels like to be the subject of the relentless pursuit of God's love.

Yes, God is a stalker in the best way possible.

Can you believe it? Do you know that He is continually present with you? He never leaves you and is well-acquainted with even the most minute details of your life. He counts every tear and knows the number of hairs on your head. He knows the good and the bad and neither of these things will change his pursuit of you.

I hope this brings you comfort. If you are feeling alone in your mess or doubting that God is right there in the midst of it,

I have two things for you to do:

1. Hold on to the truth.

Pull out your Bible and find a scripture that supports the truth about God's unwavering love for you. Look for one that really resounds in your spirit. There are some good ones in this chapter. Now, write this down, and keep it in front of you. Say it out loud every single time life tells you otherwise. Memorize it, and let it sink deep into your spirit until you fully believe it.

2. Let go of stuff.

Let it go. Yes, I know it's a popular song from a very famous movie, and it is so true. Ask God to show you the things that you are still holding on to that are keeping you tied to your mess. It could be money, it could be stuff, it could be hatred or anger or jealousy or fear of loss, but whatever it is, trust that God can deal with it, and let it go.

*"It's not what you are that holds you back,
it's what you think you are not."*
— Denis Waitley

Chapter 7

LIVE WITH EXPECTATION

LIVE WITH EXPECTATION
You are not the plus one.

Have you ever been invited by someone else to be their plus one at a really great event? Maybe it was a wedding or private party. You know what it feels like to walk in the room, thankful you were included, but knowing you were simply along for the ride.

One of the most common challenges for ex-messies as they move into a new normal life is the feeling of being a career second-class citizen. In essence, they are thankful to be in the room, but they really don't feel like they belong. If this resonates with you, repeat after me, "I am not the plus one. I have my own invitation."

I mean it. God has personally invited you to this party called life. You are not along for the ride, and His invitation is abounding with blessings. It is centered upon His deep and abiding love for you. Don't ever let yourself believe differently.

I would have lost heart, unless I had believed
That I would see the goodness of the LORD In the land of
the living
(Psalm 27:13 NKJV)

This is important. It is your defense against the enemy who will remind you that your life is messy and you have no right to expect anything more. You might as well settle. You might as well realize that this is the best you can do. You blew it.

There is no plan B in the Kingdom of Heaven.

As far as God is considered, there is no second best or backup plan for your life. He didn't bring you this far to give you a seat at the kids table. God's restorative work is complete, and it lacks nothing. In fact, as we see it in the Bible, His restoration is always abundant and filled with more than you can ask for or imagine.

This was a tough one for me. I had wasted so many opportunities, and there were aspects of my life that I believed were beyond recovery. I had missed my chance at going to college and consequently, in my brain, having a career. I was now a divorced, single mom, straight out of the bar and the drug world. I was broke and broken.

Don't get me wrong, I was thankful to no longer be stalked by a crazy man. I was growing in my relationship with God and beginning to heal from the trauma of the past few years. I simply believed that because of my past, I shouldn't expect anything more.

It was clear that my theology was a bit messy, too, and it kept me from fully entering the community at church. For starters, hanging around church social situation always cultivated feelings of illegitimacy. I felt like a fraud. I was living under a number of falsely assumed consequences surrounding my past which based upon my limited experience with church people, I believed disqualified me from ever legitimately belonging. As I have already shared, history had shown me that church was not a place equipped to handle messy people. I figured if I were ever going to fit in at church, my lifestyle had to completely change, so I committed to a strict set of self-imposed rules for how I would behave:

No men. No missing church. No messing up.

The people in church continued to be very confusing for me. Everyone was so welcoming – especially Pastor Zac. I still could not understand why he wanted me in church, along with all the other very non-Christian, worldly people who hung out at the gym. I didn't want to frustrate his grace, and make him regret his decision, so I thought that the best thing for me to do was to keep my expectations in check, try not to stand out, not let too many people know the sordid details of my past, and avoid anything that even looked like a romantic relationship at all cost.

No men. No missing church. No messing up.

To the best of my ability, I kept my church life very separate from my personal (out-of-church) life which turned out to be very unwise for many reasons I don't have time to discuss. Suffice it to say, that strategy was flawed. I kept waiting for the moment when someone would realize who I really was and sit me down so they could lay out the rules for my future. This time, I was prepared to accept them, even if it meant being second string my whole life. I was committed and remember pride has no place in surrender. Oddly enough, that moment never happened. In fact, it was exactly the opposite.

I was encouraged to join a small group in the women's ministry. I now fondly refer to them as the kitchen ladies. I don't think I am exaggerating when I say, most of them were in some process of remodeling something in their house. For most, it was their kitchen, hence the name kitchen ladies. They must have been the only over 50-year-olds in this very young, very hip, church whose three thousand members all seemed like they were under 25 years old. My group felt like a safe place where I could grow and be honest about what I was going through. I am sure that my weekly answers to the how-are-you-doing question blew their mind, but they never let on. They corrected me when I needed it, listened patiently to my story, and empathized with the drama of living with a crazy stalker. They prayed for me and encouraged me. In true kitchen lady fashion, they even crocheted little bookmarks for my Bible, baked me cookies and gave me hand-made cards with scriptures that, "I should remember." I have to admit, the normalcy of their lives drove me a little crazy, but I was committed, and I can now see the absolute brilliance of it.

In the time we spent together, I learned a lot about what a normal healthy Christian life looked like. I got a picture of what a normal healthy, Christ centered marriage looks like and received great instruction on how to be a normal, loving mother who raises her child in the way he should go. I also learned that I should never, ever remodel my kitchen. The most important thing was that I continued to grow and to learn what it meant to walk out the commitment I made that day on my knees. "For the rest of my life, I will serve only you."

I remember once asking the pastor why I was put in a group with all the old ladies. Clearly, I was not in their demographic. His response resounded in my spirit. "You are a strong leader. If I were to put you in a group of young women, you would have led them straight to the bar. You are where you belong right now, with a group of mature women who will love you enough to not let you lead them."

You are a strong leader. What? That was a new thought.

After a while, someone decided it was a good idea for me to take the next step and start serving. An opportunity came up for me to join the junior high ministry – which sounded completely awful. Besides, who in their right mind would allow someone with a past like mine to be around kids? These were some crazy church people. I reluctantly made a call to the leader, who told me to go ahead and show up to their next meeting if I was serious. I thought he was a bit rude, but again, I was committed so I agreed to, as he put it, show up. After all, I had literally faced death, how scary could it be to face a bunch of junior high people?

A few days later, I walked into the building and ran straight into a bunch of young, rather chatty and way too energetic, girls. They were happy to introduce me to their leader, Mike, who was the nicest person they had ever met. Really? I had thought he was kind of rude.

There was a concert going on that night, and I noticed that Mike was paying an exceptional amount of attention to me, even though there were other leaders and a million kids. He kept staring at me and following me around, and I could sense there might be just too much interest on his part. I was trying my best to avoid him but having no luck. By the end of the night, I was tired of the chase and decided to blurt out the one thing I believed had to be a deal breaker in the heart of this church person and nicest Christian guy ever.

"I am divorced, and I have a four-year-old son."

I braced myself, waiting to see his expression of interest change, and quite possibly be told that junior high ministry might not be a good fit for me. His response took me by surprise, as all he said was, "Cool. Can't wait to meet him."

I would later learn that he was a committed "non-dater" and for four years, had been fasting and praying for the woman

God wanted him to marry. Well, there had to be some sweet, Christian, virgin, not- messed-up girl in this church of 3,000 single people who would love to be his prize. It certainly wasn't me. Besides, he was not at all my type... way too nice.

No men. No missing church. No messing up.

Serving in the junior high ministry turned out to not be horrible, and surprisingly Mike and I became the best of friends. Along with his work with the kids he was, as they called it, a mini-church pastor which meant he led a mid-week bible study group that met in someone's home. I surprised even myself when I accepted his invitation to join it.

As our friendship grew, I shared the craziness of my past and confided in him about the man who sometimes showed up at church and sat in the row behind me. There were even a few occasions when I would call him, hysterical, because the stalker was on his way to my house in a drug-induced rage, threatening to kill me. Mike would drop everything to drive across town to sit with me, pray with me, and do the best he could to help me feel safe. What was he thinking?

People began to talk. We were always together, but there was nothing romantic going on. The kids kept saying, "You should like Mike. I think he likes you." Gotta love junior highers I tried as hard as I could to convince them and myself that he wasn't dating, and I wasn't an option – or at least, that is what I assumed.

There was no way this guy could fast and pray for four years and have God send him someone like me. That would be ridiculous.

The pressure of public opinion both from the adults and the kids was growing uncomfortable for me so I decided to have a DTR (define the relationship) talk with Mike. I needed to let him off the hook and tell him I had no expectations of being in a romantic relationship with him, or anyone for that matter. The conversation didn't go the way I had planned, because what Mike decided to tell me that night sent me into a crisis of belief:

"The moment I saw you, God said to me, 'If someone would really love her, she would be amazing.'" He confessed his feelings and said that night, he had stopped praying for God to show him who he should marry and had been praying for God to confirm it was me.

I cried all the way home, and the next day, decided to break his heart. The person he was praying for could not be me. I assumed that my past had disqualified me from ever considering such a thing. Besides, he was going through the ordination process at church and was destined to be a pastor. I did not intend to mess that up.

No men. No missing church. No messing up.

I had to let him off the hook and tell him that it would be impossible for us to be in a relationship. I was not about to be the reason why he was disqualified from his calling in ministry. What he deserved was a nice, totally pure, Christian girl who wasn't dragging around a four-year-old, a stalker, and a suitcase full of painful history. I told him he would thank me later.

My words did nothing to deter him. We had a clarifying conversation about our church doctrine of forgiveness and restoration, and the fact that one of the pastors and a few other leaders in the church had gone through divorce and were now remarried – which explained a lot. The bottom line was that I believed my past made me second-class, while Mike believed my past made me stronger.

Over the next few months, we would continue to struggle with this issue. Him, believing we were supposed to be together, and me, insisting that I would never be good enough for him. It was the only thing we ever disagreed on.

I stubbornly began praying and asking God to give me the strength to completely walk away from him, even from the friendship. It would hurt, but I was committed. Instead, as I opened my heart in prayer, God began to show me that He had no plan B for my happiness. I was not second choice, the next best thing, the charity case. I was the best, the prize, Mike's heart's desire. I eventually committed to God that if Mike Schaecher would ever ask me to marry him, I would do the smartest thing I had ever done and say yes.

No missing church. No messing up.

Three months later, in the midst of a winter rain-storm,

walking along the beach under an umbrella, Mike got down on his knee and pledged, "If you will marry me, I will love you. I will never treat you harshly, or yell at you, and I will take care of you and Josh for the rest of my life."

I said yes. He kept his word.

For over three decades, Mr. Schaecher has loved me and my son unconditionally. He has shown kindness, respect, and has not once been harsh with me. He has never yelled at me, nor handled any situation with cruelty. That is not to say that he has not been mad, frustrated to the point of crazy, or perfect in his behavior. I still had a lot of healing to walk through, and it was hard work, but I was committed, and so was he.

As for missing church and messing up, I have also learned that I have the grace to do both.

Living with assumed consequences and self-imposed regulations was an art form for me. In truth, it was a toxic coping mechanism that I used to guard my heart and keep me safe from disappointment. It would take some time and healing for me to be able to step boldly into a life of grace filled expectation and stop living as though I had just snuck into the party through heaven's back door. I am so thankful for Pastor Zac, my kitchen ladies, that horde of junior highers and Mike for being tangible examples of God's full condemnation free, acceptance and love. It made all the difference in the world.

Do you know that God desires to bless your life in ways you cannot imagine? He has not disqualified you from living in the light of His great favor. He wants you to experience His crazy goodness. If you are a messy person, or an ex- messy, I hope you can embrace this underlying truth, pick up your invitation to God's best life, stop disqualifying yourself, and take your seat at the table.

In the next chapters, we will roll up our sleeves and dig in a little deeper into some of the internal processes that God used to help me restore the broken pieces of my emotional and spiritual life. My story would not be complete without that.

For now, you can start by doing three things:

1. Accept your invitation.

> You are not a fraud; God is inviting you to live like you belong. You and God might have differing views of your value, but God is asking you to agree with Him.

2. Adjust your expectations.

> What areas are you living with assumed consequences, rather than expectation of blessing? I dropped out, so I will never finish school. I gave away my virginity, so I can never experience the blessing of purity. What nice Christian guy wants a girl with a past? You haven't lost your chance at ministry, career, relationship, love, business, or anything else

that comes to mind. God can redeem it all. It may not look the way you initially dreamed, but His restorative work is always better than you can imagine.

3. Embrace Restoration

God will restore the years the locust has eaten. He will make all things new. He will give beauty for ashes. He will turn your mourning into dancing. Stop disqualifying what God has restored. Jesus bled and died for that. He died for the best things that could ever happen to you, and it would be such a shame to live a second-best life.

We cannot solve problems by using the same kind of
thinking we used when we created them.
—Albert Einstein

Chapter 8

THE AGREEMENTS
WE MAKE

THE AGREEMENTS WE MAKE

I deserve this.

You would be surprised how much pain a person will endure simply because they have chosen to agree with these three words. The agreement creates a mindset, and the mindset becomes your reality. It will convince you that you must endure the mess, and that you don't deserve help. It will silence your voice and quench any hope for change.

Mental agreements are beliefs that are accepted as truth and powerfully influence the way you think, act, and respond to the situations in your life. Sometimes, it only takes a simple word or action that communicates a lie, which your spirit agrees with as your reality. If there is no competing message that affirms truth, this agreement can become a dominant commentary in your life.

Negative thought agreements can often be the driving force behind your mess. They can act like a skewed, internal GPS that drives your life off-course and interferes with your ability to make decisions based upon God's inspired truth.

Sometimes referred to as toxic thinking habits or limiting belief systems, there is incredible work being done by professionals, who are much more qualified than I am to discuss the clinical nuances of the concept. I strongly encourage you to seek out more revelation on this, but for the purposes of this book, I will share my experience with an exercise that has become a critical part of my healing process.

As my journey forward unfolded, I soon realized that much of the hard work I needed to do was centered around re-shaping my internal belief systems, rather than simply changing my external circumstances.

It is for freedom that Christ has set us free. Stand firm, then, and do not be encumbered once more by a yoke of slavery.
(Galatians 5:1 NIV)

Sure, escaping the violence, coming back from financial catastrophe, giving up drugs and alcohol, and healing the broken relationships with my family were things that needed to happen and happen quickly. What was equally important, was my need to identify the mental agreements I had made that were negatively influencing my decisions and had driven me to create my mess in the first place. If these were not dealt with, it would have been too easy for me to fall back on faulty directives in my life and re-create the mess I had just been set free from.

As I discussed in the previous chapter, the process of recalculating the direction of my life required complete surrender. It was all or nothing and for me, that was the only pathway forward. I had to give God full access to my heart, emotions, and thoughts. As I grew in my knowledge of God, I learned that He and I had differing opinions about me, and He wanted me to believe Him. This required me to change the agreements I had made with simple statements – such as, "I deserve this" – because they often superseded God's truth.

It was not simply a process of learning to behave differently, or even willing myself to think differently. I had to identify the toxic agreements that were in conflict with God's perspective of me, and also deal with the genesis or roots of the issues by seeking to understand where and how they originated and process those events in light of God's truth, His love and His mercy.

Dr. Caroline Leaf, author of *Switch on Your Brain* and world-renowned cognitive neuroscientist, has done incredible work in this area. She calls this process 'reconceptualizing,' and she explains the difference between this and simply training yourself to think differently in this way:

This process is different to CBT (cognitive behavioral therapy), where you are training yourself to identify the wrong thought and replace it with the correct one. You aren't simply swapping out files in your brain; you first need to find out why that 'file' was there in the first place. When it comes to reconceptualizing something, you first need to find the reason why you need to reconceptualize it… You need a reason to reconceptualize something and a reason to practice using what you have reconceptualized, and you get this from figuring out how you developed the negative way of thinking in the first place.

Today, I am thankful that people like Dr. Leaf have been able to validate with science and put words to a lot of the processes that God led me through in the early days of our walk together. Back then, none of this research was available in language that regular people could understand. I can now put language to the process that the Holy Spirit led me through as I opened my heart and submitted both my emotions and thoughts to him. It now makes beautiful sense to me.

What were you thinking? As I worked through the process of healing, this question often came up. My answer was always some form of, "I deserved it. I broke my life, I believed it was up to me to fix it." It was such a lie, but I had made an agreement with it and it had become a truth that really skewed my internal GPS and kept me trapped in a cycle of silence and isolation. This was one of the first things I had to explore.

When the question was asked, "Why would you think that?" My response would always be, "I don't know, I have always thought that way." As it turned out, the root of this thought was an ordinary childhood experience that, oddly enough, had an extraordinarily long-term consequence.

I was a very odd child. I don't say that to be self-deprecating, but I just don't think anyone in my giant, Hispanic family really knew what to do with me. I wasn't the oldest of all my cousins, and I wasn't the youngest. I wasn't great at sports, artistic, or exceptionally good at school. I was both fearfully shy and annoyingly talkative, depending on the situation. Despite the dozens of family members who all lived within a few blocks in our small neighborhood, the thing I remember most about childhood was being alone.

Nobody really noticed how alone I was. It wasn't necessarily their fault. Finding odd, out-of-the way-places to play by myself for hours and often repeating the same action – like bouncing a ball a thousand times against a wall without stopping or making dozens and dozens of mud pies for hours on end – was not conducive to people standing in line to play with me.

I didn't often get to play with the older kids in the neighborhood. I was very uncoordinated, so traditional sports, like baseball or kickball, were not an option. I did, however, look forward to the days when all the kids would get together for a neighborhood-wide game of hide and seek, because everyone was welcomed to play, especially if you weren't very good. My grandmother's porch was always home base, and the goal of the game was to hide until you were found, then run to home base before you were tagged.

One day, my parents took delivery of a refrigerator that arrived in a very large cardboard box. Being the child that I was, I saw great potential in the arrival of that giant box, and I quickly claimed it, dragged it outside, and began working on a plan that would bring me neighborhood fame forever.

I was able to create a false bottom, which became the perfect hiding spot, and somehow convinced everyone to play hide and seek, managing not to be the first one it. Things were shaping up well, and I could imagine the moment when I would emerge victoriously out of the box and go down in hide-and-seek history. Kids think like that.

When the game began, I ran as quickly as I could and crawled into the cramped space I had created at the bottom of the box. I could hear kids running and screaming as they headed for home base, and then, I could hear people looking for me. After a while, their voices grew angry as they called for me to come out, but I would not be moved.

Their voices grew silent, but I stayed put until my body began to cramp, and I was not having fun anymore. I figured enough time had passed, and no matter what happened, I still had bragging rights forever. I crawled out of the box and headed toward my grandma's porch, anticipating the moment when I would mock everyone for not being able to find me.

Nobody was there.

Everyone had grown bored of the game and tired of looking for me. They had all gone on to other things. Who could blame them? Remember, it was not unusual for me to disappear by myself for hours at a time. They weren't being mean; they were just being kids, but children are not always able to process experiences like this with the right understanding. The message I received that day would shape my thinking for a very long time. It was a lie, and it was toxic.

"You deserve this."

"Nobody is looking for you because you are not important"

I distinctly remember standing across the street from home base and feeling the powerful impression that these two thoughts made upon my heart. It felt so true based upon the circumstances and the fact that up to that point in my life, there had been very little commentary that said otherwise. In that moment I received the words as truth and made two very dangerous mental agreements that would influence my behavior for years to come.

Imagine walking through life thinking that you deserve the bad things that happen to you when you mess up and believing that people will abandon you because you are simply not that important. Knowing my story, it is easy to understand how this toxic narrative might have influenced my reactions to the challenges I was facing and kept me from seeking the help that I needed.

Beyond this, I discovered that there were other agreements I had made as a young child that had skewed my internal GPs and had unknowingly driven me in the wrong direction.

"You talk too much."

"You are so spoiled."

These statements were probably true. I did talk, endlessly, all the time and I was probably pretty annoying. I am also certain nobody understood how my grandfather could see no fault in me and showed me incredible favoritism with his time and attention. They were unwise comments at best, made by people who I know truly loved and valued me. They just could not possibly have discerned how I was processing them and the long-term effect they would have on me.

"You talk too much," became: "Nobody wants to hear what you have to say."

"You are so spoiled," became: "You don't deserve the good things you are given, even when that is love and attention."

Not all of the agreements I made came as a result of a comment or criticism from someone else. Some were simply my own response to failure or to normal challenges that I encountered as a young woman. These became resounding voices that defined me and validated the lie that my life was a lost cause:

You will never move beyond this.

Nobody good will ever want you.

You are too much trouble.

You missed your chance.

Some of these were obvious, and I was able to easily identify them. There were others, almost indistinguishable, like a tape playing in the background of my mind that I hardly noticed. These would take a while, and if I am completely honest, I think I am still working on a few. It's a process.

...If you continue in my truth, you will know the truth
and the truth will set you free.
(John 8:31-32 NIV)

As I studied God's Word and learned more about His ways my internal GPS started to align itself with truth. This was a vital part of the process of identifying some of the more toxic agreements that had contributed to the destructive narrative in my life. The more I grew in knowledge and experienced God's love firsthand, the easier it was to identify when a thought agreement was leading me away from my God inspired destination. One of the great things about a GPS is that it will automatically recalculate your directions when it detects a wrong turn.

Recalculating

Cancelling the toxic agreements that had taken me in the wrong direction for way too long allowed me to begin recalculating the direction of my life based upon truth rather than lies. One by one I identified them, explored where they began, and reconsidered them in light of God's Word and His love for me. I was then able to forgive myself and those involved for creating the situation in the first place. Only then was I able to replace that agreement with a new life narrative based upon God's truth which I could trust to lead me forward in the right direction.

I now know that I no longer deserve the punishment for my

sin, because Jesus took that upon himself. That is all to His glory.

I now know that my life is important, and it matters to God and to the people in my life who love me.

I now believe that God created me to be loved and to receive loving attention from people that validates my worth.

I still talk a bit too much, but God has given me some important things to say.

If any of this resonates with you, I encourage you to explore the possibility that you could be acting upon toxic mental agreements and as a result following faulty internal directions that are in opposition to God's inspired truth about you. This continues to be a process that really works for me. It makes sense for how I am wired, but I am certain that there are other similar processes available to you which can be equally effective. The important thing is that you begin the process of figuring that out and now would be a really great time to start.

Here are three commitments you will need to make:

1. Get in the Word.

You must have a competing voice of truth as the foundation for your internal GPS system. As you commit your heart and mind to the truths that are found in Scripture, they will become a hedge about your heart and mind and help you to identify the agreements you have made that are taking your life in the wrong direction.

2. Get Insight.

Ask the Holy Spirit to help you by revealing the agreements you have made that war against God's opinion of you or His plan for your life. Take some time to explore their origin to figure out why they exist. Forgive those involved, especially if it is yourself. Replace the toxic agreements with truthful God inspired narratives.

3. Get help.

The process I have described here is complex and can be emotionally and mentally very challenging. You will need help. Find someone who is experienced such as a licensed counselor, or a pastor willing to work with you as you take your first steps of discovery.

It is also wise to have a friend in your life who is mature in their faith and willing to say, "Really? You think that? Because that doesn't even sound like God." Find someone you can trust and give them permission to, "Call it out as they see it."

I once was lost but now I'm found, was blind but now I see.
— John Newton

Chapter 9

RECLAIM WHAT WAS LOST

RECLAIM WHAT WAS LOST

No child ever dreamed of growing up to be a drug dealer.

Instead of prince charming, can you imagine a little girl planning for the day when she would grow up and marry someone who screams at her and beats her, or little boys who can't wait until the day they become an alcoholic?

I think we can all agree that doesn't happen, and yet, sometimes, despite all the dreaming we do as little kids, some of us still manage to grow up and get lost in the process. We can contemplate the reasons why, but there usually isn't one simple answer.

What I know is that there is God-inspired destiny seeded in the hearts of our children that inspires their dreams of a promising future. This is the substance of Jeremiah 1:5 and the inspiration of Psalm 139:13

Before I formed you in the womb, I knew you, before you were born, I set you apart...
(Jeremiah 1:5 NIV)

For you created my inmost being; you knit me together in my mother's womb.
(Psalm 139:13 NIV)

Before you were even one cell, God intimately knew you and envisioned a destiny for you, according to the inspiration of His heart. And with that in mind, every physical and emotional attribute was perfectly formed to enable you to live out this inspired destiny. All this, before you ever took one breath, and certainly before you ever had the ability to mess it up.

This is the inner knowing you sensed as a child. It remains fixed in your heart, no matter how many mistakes you have made, or in some cases, how badly the people around you have failed. It is the spark inside of you that refuses to be extinguished: the thing that inspires you to keep dreaming when everything in you wants to give up.

This is the voice of God calling you back to reclaim your inspired destiny.

I know it well. Even as a child, I could sense a calling to something important. I still do. I know you do, too. Your life might not look like anything you used to dream about. Things might have gone all sorts of wrong, but this is true. God knows the plans he has for you and He will not change His mind about it.

You can't mess that up.

For a long time, I believed the lie that my life was broken beyond repair. There were things that I absolutely believed I could never recover from. These are the secrets hidden in the mess of messy people. The selfish, dark and seemingly unforgivable things that occupy territory in our mind and remind us over and over that our lives will always bear the marks of their disgrace.

In addition to exploring the mental agreements discussed in the previous chapter, this is *why* I found that it was beneficial to explore and gain an understanding of the events that led me to that crashing plane. What I eventually came to believe is that it wasn't so much about *what* went wrong—that was obvious. For me, one of the keys to healing was understanding the *how*.

The Bible teaches us that without vision, the people perish. It also says that hope deferred will make your heart sick. This is the *how* I discovered as I sought understanding of the mess I made of my life.

Where there is no vision, the people perish
(Proverbs 29:18 KJV)

Hope deferred makes the heart sick, but a dream fulfilled
is a tree of life.
(Proverbs 13:12 NLT)

How did things get so messy?

My dad came to America from Mexico as a young teenager. He was the third in a family of 13 children whose father had abandoned them, moving on to build a new family, and leaving them without any support. Talk about a messed-up situation. My grandma, who will forever be my hero, understood that their hope for a brighter future would be to get everyone to the United States. The three oldest children—my father being one of them—were sent to live in California and find a way to provide a life for their mom and siblings. For a while, they lived in the backyard of a family friend, cooked outside, and slept in a chicken coop. My dad was 14 years old and had no formal education, but he was smart and scrappy. Together with his brother and sister, they soon succeeded in bringing their family to America and carving out a better life for themselves.

My parents married quite young, and neither of them graduated from high school. Between the two of them, I had 17 aunts and uncles who, for the most part, all lived in the same neighborhood and in very close proximity to one another. Though I only had one sister, cousins were plentiful, and with so many kids in my extended family, it was easy to get lost in the crowd.

The culture I grew up in was one of hard work and family commitment, but there were also things that that were less-than-healthy. Poverty, alcoholism, drug addiction, gang violence, teen pregnancy, abuse of every kind, and a host of other destructive influences which were so prevalent, I considered them to be a normal part of life.

Despite all of this, I somehow knew I was destined to live differently, to do something important – something significant for the world. That is quite ambitious for a kid being raised in an environment like mine. As a teenager this drove me to succeed. I was the straight-A student, the cheerleader, the championship runner, the kid who wrote articles for the local paper. I insisted upon believing that I was destined for success, so in my mind, there was no room for mistakes or failure.

There was ample opportunity for me to hang out with the kids from my neighborhood who were involved with the gangs, but I chose instead, to make my social circle from who I considered to be "good kids" that lived on the more affluent side of town. I intentionally kept my home life and social life very separate. In fact, my best friends rarely ventured into my neighborhood and never visited my home. Very few knew my parents, nor had a clue what was going on in my life after I waved goodbye and headed home to the other side of the tracks.

Finishing high school was a big milestone in my family. Beyond that, getting a good job and being able to pay the bills was considered great success. My school friends all seemed to know or at least have a plan for what they would do beyond high school that included college and a vision for their future career. I had great success in high school competing in cross country and in track and everyone believed I had a shot at competing in college. That sounded like a good plan, but I had no clue how to navigate that process. It never dawned on me to ask for help.

Staying away from anything I had determined to be dangerous – like drinking, drugs, and especially, sex was a goal and almost a badge of honor for me. Teenage pregnancy was rampant in our culture, and I was determined not to become the next statistic. I was doing a pretty good job of holding it all together and admittedly pretty prideful about my success until I began my senior year of high school. It was here that things started to unravel.

That summer before school started, my dad moved us out of the neighborhood that I had grown up in all my life. This was meant to be an upgrade and should have been a good thing, but home-life was cycling out of control and now, there was no family around to notice and no grandma's house across the street to run to when things got too explosive. My dad was drinking a lot and not in a good emotional state. My mom, who was angry about having to leave her family, was fighting depression. My sister had moved out of the house and both parents were so lost in their own pain that they were completely disconnected and unaware of anything that was going on with me.

When my dad moved us across town, I learned that I was supposed to change high schools and compete for a rival team. I would no longer be allowed to compete for my school. There was no way I was doing that, so I made a deal with my school counselor and promised that if I could at least stay for my senior year, I wouldn't compete for the rival school. I was furious about the move, but never spoke a word about it to my parents and decided to do the one thing that would probably make my father the angriest. I quit running and I became a cheerleader. That did not go over well at all and only served to fuel the fire that was out of control at home. Consequently, I worked all summer to pay for the uniform, picked up my pom poms and began my senior year with no plan for how I would succeed besides my default; just try to be the best at things and don't mess up.

During this time, I started a relationship with a man four years older than I was. He had his own place, and I would often end up there when I didn't have the strength to go home and face the challenges of dealing with family life. He was charming and charismatic, and I was young and very naïve. When I confided in him about how bad things were at home, he gave me a key to his house, offering me what he called, a safe place to go when things got too crazy. It didn't take long for the relationship to escalate to a point where we started sleeping together. As quickly as that happened, I ended up pregnant.

I was devastated. What part of "just don't mess up" did I not understand? Considering that I had made a commitment to myself to steer clear of any relationships that would lead to a sexual relationship, this felt like the ultimate life fail. To make matters worse, I knew if my dad ever found out, well I couldn't let myself even consider that option. In my very immature, 17-year-old brain, I determined that the only thing left for me to do was to hide it and try to make the best of things.

Don't mess up, and if you do you better hide it.

I told nobody but the father and without even thinking about any other options, we chose to abort the baby. A good majority of my girlfriends had been through it, some multiple times. On some occasions, I was actually the one to drive them to the clinic. I never considered it peculiar that as soon as it was over, there was never any mention of it again. I never saw any tears or sensed any remorse. Everyone seemed to get back to life as if nothing had ever happened. I assumed I would do the same.

The day of my appointment there was something inside telling me not to continue to go down that road. As we drove to the clinic, I could sense the danger signs flashing, warning me to turn around and go another direction but, I believed I had no other choice. I couldn't let anybody know how I had failed.

The moment it was over, I knew that I had done something terribly wrong. Sure, I was relieved that nobody would ever know about the pregnancy, but it felt like my heart was broken in a million, irreparable pieces. Is this how the other girls really felt or am I just weak, I wondered?

What do you do with that kind of pain?

Convinced that I had no right to be sad about it because it was my choice, the pain was buried, the guilt pushed away, and a commitment was made to never speak of it again. This would be a secret nobody could ever know. Sadly, it wouldn't be my last.

I graduated one month later without anyone ever knowing

what I did.

As much as I thought I had left it in the past, this now defined the new commentary of my life: the first line item on my résumé. She tried, she failed, and then, she hid it. She is a fraud, and she will never move beyond this. Mental agreements made. I put on the appropriate filters and went on with my life.

Summer came and most of my friends were moving on with their plans to attend college and do something with their lives. The guilt of what I had done and the lack of any other plan, drove me to make the decision to marry. I was only 17 and I knew it was a mistake, but at least it was a plan for the future. Be married.

We were married a few months after graduation and within six months I was pregnant. Neither of us were ready to be parents, but I was resolved to do my best and make it work. Two weeks before my 19th birthday, I gave birth to a beautiful baby boy. Add to the plan--be a mom.

We tried to make the marriage work, but we were both too broken and immature to live out the commitment. Soon after the baby was born, he walked away to a new relationship, leaving me with a two-month-old, wallowing in the pieces of more failed plans.

I broke. The pressures of being alone, having a baby at 19, being post-partum, not having a job or a means to support us, and having no plan for a future, was a bit more than I could cope with. Looking back now, I realize that I had no healthy coping mechanism for dealing with failure or this kind of pain. My family never dealt with their problems out in the open. Denial was a strong family trait – as was suppression, pushing it away, and diversion – find something else to do, so you don't have to think about it.

Without a toolkit to process what had happened, I spiraled into a whole new level of crazy. I tried to keep it together for a while, mostly for the sake of my son. I saw a counselor; whose best advice was to quote a poem on his wall about loving something and setting it free. I never went back. As I described in chapter four, I even went to church for about a minute, which did not work for me at all and without any other options, I think I just gave up.

Hopelessness is a breeding ground for disaster.

Seeking to numb the pain, I sought out people whose lives seemed just as messy as mine. I got a fake ID, walked into my first bar, and ordered a drink. Momentary pleasure became my drug of choice. Hopelessness drowned out the voice of destiny, and by the age of 22, I found myself living the life you read about in chapter one of this book.

Understanding God's inspired destiny is a powerful coping mechanism for failure.

Someone once asked me to give them one parenting tip that contributed to my kids' success. I didn't even have to think about it. My kids know that they were created for a purpose, and that they have a God-inspired destiny. Their lives mean something. This allows them to stand strong when they fail or make a mistake. Even if they discover that they are really bad at something, they have an overriding narrative that tells them that these things do not define them. In the Schaecher family, we jokingly call this, 'an overdeveloped sense of awesomeness.'

Having a life plan that was primarily based upon not messing up was a recipe for failure. Add to this the narrative of toxic mental agreements discussed in the last chapter along with a lack of healthy coping mechanisms, and it is easy to see how things unraveled.

Understanding opened the door to forgiveness.

Gaining an understanding of how these factors worked together to influence my decisions was very cathartic. It helped me to stop the destructive narrative of self-condemnation, and though it would take some time before I was healthy enough to tackle some of the deep work surrounding issues – like the abortions – I was eventually able to receive God's complete forgiveness and heal. This paved the way for me to forgive myself, and consequently, the people in my life who had not always acted in my best interest.

You may be reading this and wondering if you will ever be able to rekindle the dreams of your childhood or feel hope again in your heart. I assure you that you can. God has never stopped believing in His plan for your life and it is time for you to reclaim your God-inspired destiny.

Here are two things that will help get you started:

1. Seek to understand the past.

There is a difference between dwelling on the past with a heart to convict and seeking to understand the past with a heart to forgive. Submit your past to God. Ask Him to give you understanding that will help you to forgive yourself and those who have hurt you. Then, let it go and watch how fast your heart can heal.

2. Reclaim your God-inspired destiny.

Take some time to recapture those dreams and visions that you had for your life when you were younger. Write them down or tell someone. Submit them to God, dare to believe, and let Him restore the hope of them.

In the moment of crisis, the wise build bridges,
the foolish build dams.
– Nigerian Proverb

Chapter 10
MESSY PEOPLE

MESSY PEOPLE

Someone in my life is messy, and I feel powerless to change it.

It is a slightly different version of the statement I made in the first chapter of this book, but one I think most everyone can relate to. This might be the only reason you picked up this book. It might even be the only chapter you thought you would read. Let me encourage you, if you haven't read the whole story, you should. The insight into the thought processes of a messy person will be incredibly valuable as you make decisions about how you can effectively manage your relationship with someone who is stuck in a destructive life cycle.

If you have a messy person in your life, you know it can be challenging, frustrating, and in some cases, absolutely heartbreaking. Finding the best way to care for them can often be quite confusing, and though there is no one-size-fits-all solution, there are a few things you can do right now that can help. The most important thing begins with you. You must settle your mind on this truth.

You are not a victim to the messy people in your life.

Let me make one thing very clear as we tackle this subject. I am speaking to adults who have the ability to choose who they allow in their life, spend time with, and invest in. This has to be clear, because as an advocate for those who don't have the ability to make these choices, and who are truly victims of some very messed-up people and systems, I never want to downplay or marginalize their situation. In fact, quite the opposite: I want to inspire you to this purpose. Find them and help them. If you can't do this directly, find the one who can, and support them.

With that said, let's get back to the business of you.

You must stop acting like you have no choice. I believe until you change this one thing, you will not be able to effectively love the messy people in your life. The truth is, you get to choose how you spend your time, energy, and resources, and you get to set the emotional and practical boundaries for all of your relationships – even the messy ones. Once you accept this, you will no longer be a victim to their life choices, and you will find a much healthier and greater joy in your relationship.

Victimization wars against collaboration.

Collaboration, simply put, is the process of people working together to achieve a goal. Being a victim will stop you from effectively working together in a healthy way, because it places you in a position of powerlessness. This is often the attitude that discourages people who are trying their best to love someone whose mess seems to be constantly spilling over into their lives. They feel stuck and are resentful of the fact that they must bear the burden of the consequences brought about by the poor life choices of someone they care about.

It often sounds like this:

"My kid is messing up so bad, but what else can I do? I can't put him out on the street."

"I have no choice. My husband is violent and drinking every day, but if I leave, he will only get worse."

"I had to loan my friend money, again, to keep her from being evicted."

You may have heard these statements, or some just like them, far too often in your life. You might even be making them right now. I have one word for you: STOP! Stop thinking this way. Now, I am not saying that you shouldn't stay with them, pay their bills, or let them move in one more time. That decision is up to you. What I am saying is that you get to choose to do these things, and once the choice is made, you are no longer a victim to it.

One of the most common questions I get asked by people seeking counsel for how to deal with a messy person is, "Should I...?" followed by the current pain point they are feeling in their life.

"Should I drive them everywhere, because they lost their license?"

"Should I pay their rent, because they will be homeless?"

"Should I quit my job to watch my grandkids, because I am worried about them?"

You get it.

The real question they are asking is, "If I do this, will it help them to get better?" The answer is probably not. These acts in and of themselves don't make messy people better. They might help them stay safe or healthy or alive for the time being. These are not bad things. But, as we have learned in the previous chapters, real change that moves you forward has to come from inside.

Deciding what to do, or deciding how to help a messy person, is not a clean process, nor is it a binary process with only two choices. I help in the manner that they ask for it, or I don't. There is a much more productive way to look at this. You can change your motivation from helping someone, to loving someone.

The goal is not to make them better: the goal is to love them.

Make love the goal. Now, the question is different: "Should I?" Well, if it communicates love and if this is important to you, then yes. I call this making a value-based decision. You get to decide what you value, and you make decisions based upon your priorities. Here is how that works: If you decide to watch your grandkids because it allows you to keep your eyes on them and ensures that they are safe, then choose that. If you choose to provide a place for your kid to sleep because having them on the streets at night is too much of a risk for you, then you get to choose that.

But remember, it is your choice, and you shouldn't punish them for it.

Continually expressing frustration at the fact that you now have to help and reminding them how angry you are, or what their failure is costing you, is not helpful to the relationship. It only cultivates shame and condemnation, and trust me, they can muster this up all on their own. More importantly, it does not communicate love. And remember, love is the goal.

Messy people take time.

It's true. The mess they are living in was probably not created overnight, and it will generally take a whole bunch of baby steps to straighten it all out. Before committing to an action, here are a few great questions to ask:

Am I committed to the long-haul process with this person?

How much time and investment am I able or willing to make?

How will this decision effect the other areas and relationships in my life?

Remember that your yes to something is always a no to a whole bunch of other things, so make sure you are considering the ripple effect of your commitment.

When I finally made the decision to leave the abusive situation I was living in, my parents did one of the most loving things they have ever done. Though they had every reason to turn me away and let me learn my lesson the hard way, they allowed me to move into their home, because they valued knowing that their grandson and I were safe and not on the streets.

Their commitment was not a carte blanche, swing-the-doors-wide- open-and-let-me-bring-my-mess-home offer. Their boundaries were clear: "We will take care of Josh and give you a place to sleep so you are safe, but nothing else."

I am certain it was not easy to watch the struggle that ensued over the next year. I had only the clothes on my back, a mountain of debt, a low-paying job, and not a dollar to my name. They could have stepped in, paid bills, purchased clothes, and made it all better, but that would not have been helpful. As it turned out, it was life-changing for me to experience both the pain and the success of putting my life back together one small step at a time.

Clear communication is the key to success.

Communication that is centered on truth and supports healthy emotional boundaries is critical. This should include three things: affirmation of who they are, communication of your values, and a clear reminder of your commitment.

Affirmation of truth.

When people find themselves caught in challenging life situations, an affirmation of who they are and a reminder that God hasn't changed His mind about them can be powerfully healing. It can help to envision them to a brighter, God-inspired future.

"I love you and believe in you, and I know that you are

going to find your way, because God has made you smart and resourceful. Remember that He hasn't changed His mind about who you are."

Communication of values.

A clear statement regarding what you value will go far to eliminate guilt in the relationship and will communicate much needed value to a person who might be struggling to love themselves.

"Right now, it is important to me that I know you are safe and have a place to sleep, or that you have proper medical care, or that you always have food, so, I would like to offer..."

Clarity of your commitment.

Clarifying your boundaries and setting realistic expectations cultivates a safe and stable environment for people whose lives feel exactly the opposite. This explains how you will collaborate or work together to help them achieve the goal of finding their way forward.

"I love you and want you to know that will not change. When you are ready to move forward, I can help in this way. In the meantime, I will meet you once a week to check in and connect with you."

Don't forget, you are changing the rules of your relationship, and that might take a bit of work. You may need to say these things over and over, and probably one more time after that. I actually ask people to write this out and practice. No matter what line you draw, you must do your best to stick to the boundaries that you set. Be confident and strong and be consistent.

Let me make a point about boundaries. If you don't have them, you will soon find that the mess of your messy person is spilling over into your world. You must decide how much access you give based upon your messy persons level of health. A word of caution: It is always easier to give more than it is to limit access already given.

There are two things I strongly suggest you consider as you attempt to set boundaries that will be conducive to maintaining a healthy relationship with a messy person:

Defend the lines of respect.

When you allow people to cross respectful lines in your relationship, it will often push you into a disconnect cycle. It looks like this: I am frustrated or hurt by how you treated me. I cut you out of my life, at least for a while, until I let you back in and you do it again; but this time, I am angrier, and the disconnect is longer.

If you don't learn to defend the lines of respect with the challenging people in your life, you will cease to like them and want them around. Remember, the goal is to love them, not fix them.

Start by communicating the expectations for your interaction with one another. When those lines are crossed, remind your messy person what respect looks like in your relationship, and let them know that you cannot allow them to act like that, because you love them and want them to continue to be a part of your life. Don't just tell them the what but help them understand the why. This is a collaborative statement that reinforces your love and commitment to the relationship.

"It is my goal for us to stay in relationship, so let's work together to make sure that happens. In the future, when we are together, I can't let you speak to me like this..."

Build a bridge of love and stay on it.

I like to use the analogy of a bridge built between your two worlds. You can stay on your side and refuse to interact with them unless they cross over and get their act together. You can cross over into their world and get immersed in the craziness and complexity of the details – which is never helpful. Or you can stand resolutely in the center, ready to remind them who they are and affirm your love and commitment to them. You have to be clear in this, "I will go this far with you, but no further." Make a commitment to stay out of the center of their mess and keep your life healthy.

A healthy you is the best person to deal with the brokenness of others.

Messy people often do not want your help to clean up their mess; they want you to help them live with it. Centering your relationship around all things wrong in their life won't help them move forward. It will consume the time that you have together and keep you from experiencing the joy of them as a person. Outside of the practical assistance you have committed to, resist the urge to become emotionally over-invested in finding solutions for them and getting your life filled up with the difficult details of their life.

This is probably one of the hardest things to do. It requires thought and intention, good communication, and so much patience. It works like this: your messy person wants to continually drag you in to the broken details of their life through conversation, complaints, or controversy. The situation sounds messy, sad, and dangerous, but you cannot go there. A simple statement that acknowledges their pain, but offers no solution, and one that reminds them of your love for them would sound like this:

"Look, that sounds hard, and I hate that you are in pain, but you will find a way to make it through. My money is on you. Let's plan to meet here again next week for lunch. Our time together is important to me."

You don't offer solutions. You don't give an opinion. You

gently refuse to cross the bridge and live in the crazy details of their life. As we discussed previously, affirm who they are, communicate your values, and clarify your commitment. That's it. The chaos of a messy person's life will spill over into yours if you cannot stay off of their side of the bridge.

Consistency. Consistency. Consistency.

This will take an incredible amount of self-control on your part, and you will repeat yourself more than you ever thought possible. As I said before, I often encourage people to write these statements out, practice them, and stick to the script. That might sound a bit drastic, but in the heat of the moment, you will be glad you did.

They may check out in frustration for a bit, and that's okay. When they check back in, move forward quickly, and repeat the same statement as before.

Consistency will pay off, and after a while, they will understand that you cannot live with them in their mess. They will also know that no matter what, you love them and are committed to the relationship. More importantly, you will feel the freedom that comes from loving them out of choice, rather than obligation, and you will be able to enjoy them again, despite the mess.

Even if they never change.

You might not be the one to help.

Messy people can be the best investment of your life or your worst nightmare. It is important to consider that maybe you're not in the best position to help.

I have to be honest, there have been times when I just had to walk away. I was not the one best suited for the journey, and though it was painful, I had to admit it.

In situations where someone poses a real threat of harm to you or your family, you must use wisdom. Access is a privilege, not a right, and you are not obligated to give destructive people access to your life, even if this is a family member. My best advice is to steer them in the direction of professional help and release them. It's okay; you may let them go. God never will. He has got them, and He will not stop His pursuit of their heart.

In my crazy, messed-up situation, God brought just the right people into my life at just the right time. This is not a knock on anyone else. There were people who tried, but they weren't the ones equipped to help at the time. My life was complicated and chaotic. It still makes me sad when I think of the people I cared about who were hurt or adversely affected by my decisions, simply because they were close to me.

Over the years, as I got healthy, some have circled back into my life, and I am so thankful for the long years of friendship we have had. Some didn't, and that's okay. I know they love me and are happy to hear that I eventually found my way forward.

Above all, I know that all who witnessed the journey, or heard of the story, or dared to be close enough to watch it play out, know, beyond a shadow of a doubt, that there simply isn't a mess too big for God to handle.

I assume if you made it this far, there is a good chance you have a messy person in your life that is pulling at your heart strings. I am happy that you are still in the game. Let me encourage you to press in and don't give up. I know you will find a way to love them, even if they choose to stay messy.

Let me remind you that these three things can help:

1. Commit to love.

Remember the goal is not to help them, the goal is to love them. Make a commitment today to change the way you view your involvement in their life. God loves them with an everlasting love. Ask Him to let you join Him in His quest to help them realize it, then build a bridge of love and stay there.

2. Communicate clearly.

Get clear in your own head, what your involvement will look like. This will include support, boundaries, and expectations. Once you are clear, be intentional about clearly communicating what these are. Don't forget to repeat this often and to communicate immediately if anything changes.

3. Be consistent.

Consistency is powerful. The life of a messy person can be chaotic and unstable. Your consistency in upholding your boundaries and following through with what you communicate will create a safe space for them. They may want more, or not like what you have decided, but they will appreciate the fact that they will always know what to expect.

Beautiful are those whose brokenness gives birth to
transformation and wisdom.
— John Mark Green

THE LAST WORD

THE LAST WORD...
There really is no lost cause.

It was an all too familiar scene, complete with the bruises, tears, panic, and the terrified look of someone who is running for their life. My stomach turned at the sight of it and the thought that I would ever be involved with something like this again.

It was a normal Sunday afternoon. My husband Mike and I were on our way home from looking at model homes with our 10-year-old daughter Megan in the backseat of our very mid-life sedan. Megan loved all things decorating, so this was one of the things she and I liked to do together. Mike was along for the ride.

I am really not sure how or why I ended up in the driver's seat. I can't actually remember more than a few times that I ever drove on a family outing. For some reason, which makes sense to all of us now, I happened to be in control of the car.

We lived on a very curvy, somewhat dangerous two-lane road. There are many places where you can barely get a glimpse around the corner, and it is rare to find anyone attempting to walk along the road as there are no sidewalks or places to walk safely.

We were almost to our house when I saw her running towards us down the road. She was wearing sunglasses, but I could tell she was crying… no, she was sobbing, it was clear, she was in trouble.

As we passed her and rounded the next dangerous curve, I could see a truck pulled over on the side of the road. There is no actual place in the road where this is safe, and my spirit immediately began to connect the dots. I saw him get out of the truck and begin walking down the road towards us…towards her. It had been at least two decades since I had ever seen anything like it, but the look of rage on his face told me everything I needed to know.

"She is in trouble." I said to Mike.

"We have to help her."

In the moment, I suppose I had a choice to make. Fight or flight, right? I could have chosen flight, calling 911 safely from my home less than ¼ mile up the road, but something in me snapped. Not on my street. Not on my watch.

I chose fight.

Without waiting for a response from Mike, I quickly flipped the car around, making what Mike called later, a crazy impossible U-turn. I looked in the rear-view mirror to see the man immediately turn and race back towards his truck. Game on.

I sped towards the woman, with the ferocity of a mama bear. As we pulled up beside her, I lowered the window down on the passenger side of the car and screamed, "Do you want help?" She stopped in her tracks, looking back down the road towards where the man was pulled over. I screamed again, "Do you want help?" She couldn't speak through the panic and fear of the moment, but she shook her head yes. "Get in the car now," I screamed. She immediately swung the door open and jumped into the back seat next to Megan. I hit the gas pedal and we took off.

The man had managed to turn his giant truck around and I could see him trying to catch up to us. He didn't have much of a chance. I knew exactly what to do. I had done it more times than I could count. I knew how to use side streets and driveways to get out of sight. I knew how to stay calm and choose the best route that would keep my car moving as fast as possible. Sadly, I knew how to get away from a violent raging man who would stop at nothing to catch me.

She was crying so hard she could barely talk. I had her put her seatbelt on and told her she was safe. I am quite sure she did not believe me at first. I clearly didn't look anything like a woman who was capable of dealing with more than the rush of an after-Christmas sale at the mall. I assured her I knew what I was doing, that I had done this before. We would get away. I had experience with these kinds of men. She fastened her seatbelt and removed her sunglasses. One glance in the mirror told the story. I could see the bruising around her eyes and cheeks and the look on her face of shame broke my heart. Tears were stinging my eyes, but I kept it together and drove like her life depended on it, because it did. "It's going to be okay." I yelled from the backseat. As we took off, I began to tell her my story.

"Many years ago, I was involved with a drug dealer..."

Instinct had taken over and I drove like a woman possessed, all the while continuing to blurt out the unimaginable details of my life that somehow made me exceptionally qualified for this moment.

He was abusive

Plane crash

Rescued

Stalked

Car chases

Mike was there at the end

Kidnapped

Broken

Freedom

There was no chance this guy was going to catch us. The windy road had almost no places to turn off, so I silently prayed that God would open up the road in front of us and put enough distractions in his way to stretch the distance between us. It was easier when we got out to the main road and I was able to lose him putting enough distance between us to feel safe.

I drove around for an extra-long time just to be sure I was completely out of harm's way before I stopped the car letting Mike get in the driver's seat which made him breathe a sigh of relief.

I went to jump in the backseat with the woman remembering in that one horrific moment that oh yes, she was sitting next to Megan. Oh my gosh, Megan.

Our youngest child sat in the backseat of the car in absolute shock. Besides, the obvious picking up a hysterical woman by the side of the road and being chased by a crazy man in a truck, I knew her enough to know she was having a hard time processing the story. The look on her face expressed the real question in her mind. "Who are these people I thought were my parents?" She knew nothing of my past. Of course, Joshua knew, he lived through it. My second son Phillip, who Mike and I had two years after we were married knew a little because he had heard me on occasion speak at churches or at conferences. I had not actually gotten around to telling my baby girl. As far as she knew, we were her very square, nothing exciting, overly protective, mostly boring, youth pastor, parents.

I asked Megan to jump in the front seat and I climbed into the backseat with the woman. Mike began making some calls to organizations that specialized in these kinds of things and arranged for help while I listened to the woman's story. This man was her husband, but he was violent and abusive. She had no way to get free from him. They had two sons and he was threatening to take them away from her. She had no family living nearby and she had no friends she could turn to. I shared my testimony with her, the part about God and His transformative work in my life and let her know there was no doubt in my mind that God loved her and had just done a miracle in her life by putting us together on that road.

There are no coincidences in heaven.

We prayed together, thanking God for keeping us all safe and asking him for a solution to the problem. After a few phone calls we were able to get her accepted into a nearby rescue center. She would be given shelter, counseling and there was a donor who would be able to fund an airplane ticket to get her and her kids to her parent's house in another state when the time was right. We dropped her off at a safe house, confident she was in good hands knowing that God had truly intervened in her life in a way that was pretty miraculous.

As we drove away from the shelter, Meg was back in her seat in the back of the car, still in shock and I could tell still trying to make sense of what just happened. For a while I let her sit in silence. She is that kid that doesn't need a lot of words. Eventually, I broke the ice saying, "Honey, I am sorry that you had to find out that your mama lived a crazy, messy life, stalked by a drug dealer, addict, crazy man who was trying to kill her and your daddy helped her get free and then married her. "

We don't have to talk about it now, but when you are ready, I will answer any questions you have." I added.

"It's okay mommy." Was all she said.

Two weeks later, while driving down the road calmly and at

the speed limit, I might add, she brought it up. "I am ready to talk about it now" she said. And so, we did.

This was her first face to face encounter with this kind of tragedy. It made my heart overflow with thankfulness that the world I came from, filled with so much violence and pain was so foreign to her. She had some questions about my life, not many. They were mostly about the obvious disparity between who she thought her mama was now, and who I used to be. The truth came easily because it affirmed the great and transformative work God had done in my life.

She was mostly moved by the fact that we were able, and willing to help this woman and said that she hoped when she grew up, that God would give her opportunities to do the same, just like her mama. I reminded her, as I often did, that God had incredible, things for her to do and assured her, jokingly, that I would be happy to pay for her counseling when she grew up so she could deal with the trauma of being chased by a madman, while her mom told the unbelievable story of how God saved her from a very messy life.

If a man has a hundred sheep and one of them gets lost,
what will he do? Won't he leave the ninety-nine others in the
wilderness and go to search for the one that is lost
until he finds it?
(Luke 15:4 NIV)

I guess the point of the story is this. God's love will always find you. You are never too lost, or too broken or too hidden. You could be in a plane, crashing to the ground, or running down a windy road on a Sunday afternoon. Regardless of where you find yourself, He is there. He is always there.

My life is proof that no one is beyond His reach. Nobody would have bet on me, including me. Nobody knew how to stop the crash that was coming, and it came. But God reached down into the wreckage of my life and He saved me. I am the girl who fell from the sky and lived to talk about it. Even now, over three decades since I walked away from that plane holding my one muddy, messy shoe, I am still struck by the wonder of it all.

This is a true testimony of God's glory, of His revealed magnificence. Because who but God would refuse to change His mind about such a messy person? Who but God would insist upon loving and pursuing one who so clearly did not deserve it? Who but God could see the treasure buried so deeply in such a messed-up life?

He has stretched out His hand to you. Will you reach for it? The question remains. It begs an answer and will not relent. "Do you want help?" If the answer is yes, get in the car, strap yourself in and fight back. Fight for the life that God inspired for you. This is still his best plan for your life. You simply can't mess that up. Now, it's time to recalculate the direction of your life and find your way forward. I know you can do it.

I believe in miracles. I am one, so are you.

He reached down from on high and took hold of me;
he drew me out of deep waters. He rescued me from my
powerful enemy, from my foes, who were too strong for
me. They confronted me in the day of my disaster, but the
Lord was my support. He brought me out into a spacious
place; he rescued me because he delighted in me.
(Psalm 18: 16-19 NIV)

CITATIONS

Chapter 1

If the lion does not tell her story, the hunter will."
— African Proverb

God had mercy on me so that Christ Jesus could use me as a prime example
of his great patience with even the worst sinners. Then others will realize
that they, too, can believe in him and receive eternal life.
(1Timothy 1:16 NLT)

…so is my word that goes out from my mouth: It will not return to me
empty, but will accomplish what I desire and achieve the purpose for which
I sent it.
(Isaiah 55:11 NIV)

Chapter 2

Strengthfinders 2.0 test

"The Sovereign LORD has given me a well-instructed tongue, to know the
word that sustains the weary."
(Isaiah 50:4 NIV)

https://www.ancient-hebrew.org/definition/sin.htm

Finally, I confessed all my sins to you and stopped trying to hide my guilt. I
said to myself, "I will confess my rebellion to the LORD." And you forgave
me. All my guilt is gone.
(Psalm 32:5 NLT)

Chapter 3

Angelo Merindino, Bring the target closer. From an article posted on the website: https://mustbethistalltoride.com/2014/11/19/bring-the- target-closer/

"Do not despise these small beginnings, for the Lord rejoices to see the work begin..." (Zechariah 4:10 NLT)

Chapter 4

Two are better off than one for they can help each other succeed. If one person falls, the other can reach out and help. But someone who falls alone is in real trouble. (Ecclesiastes 4:9-10 NLT)

https://www.merriam-webster.com/dictionary/vulnerable

Brown, B. (2015). Rising Strong. Vermilion.

Chapter 5

Genesis 3:8-25.

"Because of the joy awaiting Him, He endured the cross, disregarding its shame." (Hebrews 12:2 NLT)

Chapter 6

"You have searched me, Lord, and you know me. You know when I sit and when I rise; you perceive my thoughts from afar. You discern my going out and my lying down; you are familiar with all my ways. Before a word is on my tongue you, Lord, know it completely..." (Psalm 139:1-4 NIV)

And we know that God causes everything to work together for the good of those who love God and are called according to his purpose for them. (Romans 8:28 NLT)

I can never escape from your spirit.

I can never get away from your presence. If I go up to heaven, you are there;

If I go down to the grave, you are there. If I ride the wings of the morning,

If I dwell by the farthest oceans,

Even there your hand will guide me, and your strength will support me. (Psalm 139:7-10 NIV)

Chapter 7

I would have lost heart, unless I had believed

That I would see the goodness of the LORD In the land of the living (Psalm 27:13 NKJV)

Chapter 8

It is for freedom that Christ has set us free. Stand firm, then, and do not be encumbered once more by a yoke of slavery. (Galatians 5:1 NIV)

Caroline Leaf, *Switch on Your Brain: The Key to Peak Happiness, Thinking, and Health* (Grand Rapids, Michigan: Baker Books, [2013])

…If you continue in my truth, you will know the truth and the truth will set you free. (John 8:31-32 NIV)

Chapter 9

Before I formed you in the womb, I knew you, before you were born, I set you apart… (Jeremiah 1:5 NIV)

For you created my inmost being; you knit me together in my mother's womb. (Psalm 139:13 NIV)

Where there is no vision, the people perish (Proverbs 29:18 KJV)

Hope deferred makes the heart sick, but a dream fulfilled is a tree of life.
(Proverbs 13:12 NLT)

The Last Word

He reached down from on high and took hold of me; he drew me out of deep waters. He rescued me from my powerful enemy, from my foes, who were too strong for me. They confronted me in the day of my disaster, but the Lord was my support. He brought me out into a spacious place; he rescued me because he delighted in me. (Psalm 18: 16-19 NIV)

THE AUTHOR

JULIE SCHAECHER

Pastor Julie Schaecher has been a ministry leader dedicated to telling her story of God's relentless love and life transforming grace for over three decades.

Following a successful career as a business owner, consultant, and destination expert in the conference management industry, Julie integrated the strategies she learned in the marketplace with the core principles of her Christian Faith, in an effort to help the church create healthier staff cultures, navigate positive change, and overcome barriers that stand in the way of their inspired vision. She currently serves as the Executive Pastor of the Movement Church in San Marcos, California.

She is the founder of the NOW Leadership Summit whose mission is to raise awareness of the value, voice, and influence of female leaders in communities around the globe where women have historically been silenced and oppressed.

After raising three beautiful children, Julie and her husband Michael are soaking up the fun of their grandma and grandpa years in beautiful Southern California.

Coming soon: 2022 AND BEYOND...

MESSY MARRIAGE- Building a winning life together.

MESSY FRIENDSHIP- Cultivating lifelong sisterhood.

Julieschaecher.com

CPSIA information can be obtained
at www.ICGtesting.com
Printed in the USA
LVHW030944161121
703456LV00008B/409